"If you're a hairdresser or salon owner, *Passionate Salon Professionals* could change your life. Using inspirational stories and a little psychology, industry experts Dr. Lewis Losoncy and Joe Santy show you how making a difference in someone else's life can make a profound difference in yours. The idea is to be passionate about what you do and to change you response to the negative energy that comes your way. The message? You can change the world, one person at a time. It's a message that resonates in these unsettling times."

—**Marianne Dougherty**
Editor in Chief, ***American Salon***

"The *Passionate Salon Professional* gives you the answer to what it takes to get a maximum career in hairdressing. Losoncy and Santy inspire you to think about your profession in a new, exciting way. Its not about the cut, its about the kindness. Our work is about people and reading these ideas will turn your job into a meaningful and passionate profession."

—**Kenneth Anders**
President, Intercoiffure, America-Canada

"How lucky the client or colleague of the stylist embracing the lessons learned in the *Passionate Salon Professional* will be. Dr. Lew Losoncy and Joe Santy have shown that the truly successful salon professional has to have so much more than great skills. This book teaches the reader to be a better person on so many levels, offering fresh approaches to difficult situations that work both inside and outside of the salon. Positive and motivational, this book coaches the reader to accept drive, heart and passion into his or her world. The *Passionate Salon Professional* is well written by two renowned industry insiders and should be read by anyone and everyone in the salon world."

—**Maggie Mulhern**
Beauty, Fashion and Markets Director
Modern Salon Media

"PSP IS THE NEW TOOL TO BE CARRIED BY THE BEAUTY PRO-FESSIONAL. With a team made up of a physiological genius and a hairdresser who have taught all over the world, you get a book that is a must read. Dr. Lew and Joe Santy have hit a grand slam. The information in *PSP* will take the ordinary beauty professional and make them extraordinary. I would make this book mandatory reading for all beauty professionals. It will be on my booklist. *PSP* rocks. I love it. I am eager to support this message because that is what beauty is really all about: passion and heart. This book has heart. A must read and reread."

—Geno Stampora
Stampora Consulting, Inc.

"I read the manuscript on my way to auditions and I really enjoyed it. Working on *American Idol* I encounter many different people from all over the United States. It is amazing how small this world is and how everyone is the same! Everywhere you go and everyone you meet has the need for acceptance, acknowledgement and appreciation. It doesn't matter if you are an A list celebrity or an A list housewife, everyone has the same needs. Being able to recognize and fulfill those needs will make you a STAR! That's what Losoncy and Santy have done for you."

—Dean Banowetz
Key Hair AMERICAN IDOL

"This is a true study guide, a real time working model you can develop to insure your client's, salon, and personal success for years to come. So, grab your pen and highlighter and walk in the footsteps of two of the most successful members of our industry."

"He who walks with the wise grows wise." (Proverbs)

—Donn Matlack
MDT - MATLACK DEVELOPMENTAL TRAININGS

"The key to a successful stylist client relationship is to understand the inside of your clients' head. Once you have achieved that the outside is easy!! That's what this book makes crystal clear."

—Nicholas French
NAHA Winner, Matrix Global Artistic Designer

"This is a book — a story — written by two very influential men in a very powerful industry. Just as the professionals who buy and read these inspiring words help to shape the lives of their clients, these men have created a book that will shape the lives of all professionals for decades to come."

—**Douglas A. Cox,**
Douglas A. Cox & Associates

"Seldom in your life do you have the great fortune to meet two individuals who have the drive, passion and dedication to make a difference in an industry and peoples life's that work in that industry. Dr Lew and Joe Santy are contagious with the energy and passion they have given our industry."

—**Bill Peel**
President, Peel's Friendly Beauty,
Xenon School of Nebraska

"As a salon owner for over thirty years, a guest artist and teacher for most of my career; and on the Logics Haircolor development team, I read *PSP* with particular interest — as it almost seemed to be a biography of myself. These are the exact emotions that have driven my passion for the industry, artistic expression, salon ownership, and most importantly, caring for people! As a leading hair colorist in the industry and Guest Artist for Matrix, I have had the privilege of knowing and working with both the authors of this book for many years. This book will be an invaluable tool for everyone interested in career success and advancing this industry for many years to come."

—**Richard Cardone**
Salon Owner,
Internationally Renowned Haircolorist

"Dr. Lewis Losoncy is the backbone of the beauty profession who, through this book with Joe Santy, inspires and encourages every cosmetologist in a salon or beauty school to believe and succeed in this beautiful profession."

—**Stacey Burk** and **Amy Ellison**
Cosmetology Instructors
Butler County Vocational Technical School

"After reading *Passionate Salon Professionals*, I felt the same as when I leave the hair salon knowing I got a great haircut; motivated, upbeat and more self-confident. The book reminds us of things we knew but somehow forgot and offers practical "how to" tips. It also gives some excellent psychological insight and some philosophy is thrown in for good measure. Santy and Losoncy quickly and efficiently get to the heart of how to become a PSP'er and explain how by doing the best job possible, success will follow. Now I know why my entire family and I have been with the same salon for all these years. It is staffed with Passionate Salon Professionals!"

—**Craig D. Weiss, Ph.D.**
CEO, Pro Performance Solutions Consulting

"In over my 20 year career as a hairstylist and educator both Joe and Dr. Lew have inspired me to strive to achieve my maximum potential as a hair stylist. Two goals that I have set out to achieve are to increase the level of professionalism in the industry and second, that we as professionals are respected. To anyone that reads this book I assure you it will elevate you to the next level. BRAVO TO JOE AND LEW."

—**Rocco Campanaro**
Salon Owner
Winner of NAHA, North American Hairdresser of the Year
Contessa Master Champion, and Canadian Hairdresser of the Year

"*Passionate Salon Professionals* is a book about the secret to becoming a great hair stylist. And yes, there is a secret! A good stylist can be taught to cut, style, and color hair, but a pro can do the same *and* create magic. There are many good stylists, but only a very few great ones. The secret is passion. Joe Santy lives a life of passion and brings that passion to his work. Dr. Lew is a highly respected psychologist. Together they instruct the reader, in practical terms, the art of becoming a PSP'er. This book is a "must read" for anyone in the salon industry who aspires to become one of the very few and who wishes to experience outstanding success in their profession."

—**Vincent M. Roazzi**
Best-selling author, ***The Spirituality of Success***

PASSIONATE SALON PROFESSIONALS (PSP)

"I cosmetically and psychologically transform self-images and destinies of fellow human beings. ... I'm a Passionate Salon Professional!"

DR. LEWIS LOSONCY
Matrix Motivational Psychologist

JOE SANTY
Salon Owner, Internationally Renowned Guest Artist

PRESS

A Division of the Diogenes Consortium

SANFORD • FLORIDA

Published by DC Press
2445 River Tree Circle
Sanford, FL 32771
www.focusonethics.com
407-688-1156

This book was set in Adobe Janson Text
Cover Design and Composition by Jonathan Pennell

ISBN: 1-932021-26-4

First DC Press Edition
10   9   8   7   6   5   4   3   2   1

Printed in the United States of America

Other DC Press Titles
by Lewis Losoncy

If It Weren't for You, We Could Get Along!
Stop Blaming and Start Living

If It Weren't for the Customer, Selling Would be Easy!

The Motivating Team Leader

Turning People On: How to Be an Encouraging Person

Retain or Retrain: How to Keep the Good Ones from Leaving

A Passion for Beauty (DVD)

Attitude Modification: Motivating Yourself Against All Odds! (6 DVD Set)

*Dedicated To
The Worldwide Community
of Passionate Salon Professionals
Who Are Changing the World,
One Client at a Time*

*To
Arnie & Sydell Miller,
Founders of Matrix.
For Making Professional Products
with A Purpose.
The Purpose of Building
Passionate Salon Professionals*

*With Love
To My Beautiful Daughter Alexa,
My Mother, Vilma Santy,
My Father, Joseph Santy,
And My Mare*

*With Love
To Diane, Gabbie, Tyler and Melissa*

Acknowledgments

TO EVERYONE AT MATRIX from Education to Marketing to Sales who are changing the world. Especially Matrix's passionate field force and design team members. To the leadership team of David Craggs, Francesca Raminella, Ketan Patel, Michael Pecce, Nick Ionnedes, Martin Dale, Cynthia Pitchford, Brooke Carlson, Karrie Fonte, Gail Cohen, Joe Sileo, Donald Culver, and Eric Mellet. To the dynamic teams at Matrix Global Academic in New York and Matrix Sales University in Paris. Our research on passion was inspired by Matrix's vision that focuses on passion. And to Matrix's great distributors and sales and store professionals.

To Dennis McClellan who is both a magician and a publisher. Dennis' caring, passion and patience has revealed to us that "PSP" transcends industries. You take an author's humble words, and turn them magically into a book… overnight! Thanks Dennis.

To Gabrielle Losoncy. You were always available for us to edit, improve, and mostly reassure us we are on the right path consistent with the approved writing style. We love you. You reminded us of the importance of vinyl in a different age. And you were 15 when you did all these things!

To Mary Mastrobuoni. You painstakingly turned Catholic School scribbling into the typed word. You're the greatest!

ACKNOWLEDGMENTS FROM LEW LOSONCY...

To Diane and Gabbie for your support, encouragement and expertise, and to my friend Joe Santy, who, for three decades, has always been there for me, fighting for my right to sing!

ACKNOWLEDGMENTS FROM JOE SANTY...

Special thanks to my friend Dr. Lew whose passion has made this collaboration a reality. He has been an inspiration to me for 30 years!

To my daughter Alexa, who keeps me young. To Mom, Dad, John, Sharon, Jim, Juli, Jimmy, and Ashley who have always been there for me.

To Mary for your support and encouragement.

To my clients and great staff at Attitudes: Joanne, Debbie, Nancy, Kelly, Roxanne, Bridget, Stefanie, Bernadette, and Nick. Your passion for our industry continues to inspire me.

A very special thanks to Pat Johnson who took a chance with a kid that was still in beauty school. I have never forgotten it and I've taken your lesson helping others to heart.

Introduction

PASSIONATE SALON PROFESSIONALS

"You may say I'm a dreamer,
but I'm not the only one;
I hope someday you will join us,
and the world will live as one."

— *"Imagine"* John Lennon

WHAT IF THE BEAUTY PROFESSION could change the world? What if your profession could do what presidents and kings have failed to accomplish throughout the centuries? Help millions of individuals feel more secure, more understood, more hopeful, more beautiful and more confident. What if every beauty professional throughout the world was gathered in one place and was committed to designing a more wonderful world by making one client at a time look and feel better? Think of the possibilities!

Sense your spiritual connection to countless other beauty artists who are touching and improving the lives of tens of millions of fellow humans everywhere. Experience yourself in your everyday role, as one of these caring experts in the worldwide network of world changers. This transformational process is going on every moment in some hamlet, village, town, and city somewhere in the world. You are never alone at your chair in the salon. You are bonded with others you never met from different cultures and languages, in the common process of making the world a more beautiful place, one person at a time.

What is that process that connects you to a world purpose? A person arrives to meet you, feeling some sort of hope for a new day. She relaxes and shares her dreams with you. You reassure her that you can help her step a little higher in life. You softly touch, soothe and cleanse her, then perform your magical artistic feats of sculpture, color, and texture, finally turning her around to open her eyes to her new world.

All of this is happening in this safe, sacred shelter, a relaxing haven known by many different names in many different places. These common sites where this world changing process is occurring we call, "salons."

Those persons who are doing hair we call "haircutters" or hairdressers or beauticians or stylists. And those who are sensing their higher purpose with their brother and sister beauty artists throughout the world we will refer to as, "Passionate Salon Professionals, or PSP's"

This book is about these PSP's, their beliefs, their attitudes, their view of their lives, their work, their profession, their clients and their teammates in the salon community.

Joe Santy, salon owner and international guest artist, walks with you through your everyday salon experiences giving you inspirational and sometimes humorous examples of the differences between "haircutters" and passionate salon professionals.

And Matrix's motivational psychologist, Dr. Lew Losoncy offers you insights from the field of psychology to keep your passionate fires alive to change the world.

YOUR PROFESSION IS IN AN EXCITING TRANSFORMATION!

You might say that we are dreamers. And we know we are not the only ones. We are in the midst of an exciting worldwide movement of salon professionals who are opening their eyes to experience so much more to their profession than just "going to a job." These highly motivated beauty artists bring their hearts into the salon to encourage, to enlighten, as well as to lighten their clients' lives. In the process they are lightening their own lives.

We are sensing salon professionals throughout the world looking for, and finding a higher view, and a deeper purpose in their life work. We are visiting with these spirited stylists, chemical specialists, aestheticians, and nail technicians everywhere. Even though they never met, these animated artists are simultaneously sensing that they aren't just changing hair colors; they are adding colors to their clients' lives. They aren't just giving perms; they are adding bounce to peoples' lives.

The passionate salon professionals are realizing they are giving people such deep gifts that go beyond cosmetics, and enter the heartier realm of touching their spirits, their confidence and their hope.

This transformational process is occurring every day in salons – every hour in some salon. And passionate salon professionals rewards come from seeing their clients smile, walk out differently than they came in, and then send in a friend later to experience the same transformation.

Yes, we are in the midst of an exciting, revolution of your profession. This book is written to encourage you to be a part of this professional transformation, because it will change your life. This change is the result of something as simple as a leap in thinking about turning your work life into your lifework resulting in an instant rise in passionate pride, purpose and prosperity in your profession.

How important is your view of your work? Perhaps it is one of the most vital factors in your view of yourself!

PASSIONATE SALON PROFESSIONALS
HAVE A HISTORY TO STYLE ON

Your profession was created as far back as the first time one person looked into another person's eyes and touched the person's hair with a caring desire to help him or her look or feel better. Your profession has evolved from that moment. The professional skills, tools, techniques and the professional products have especially exploded in the last few decades.

Something else has evolved. And passionate salon professionals realize that, "I have the possibility to change the world every moment I look into the eyes and touch the hair, skin and nails of my client." Something is going on here in your profession. You can find evidence of this revolution of your profession, first in your heart, and next, in your eyes.

In her insightful book, *The Aquarian Conspiracy*, Marilyn Ferguson concluded that we can create a new world by simply choosing a new view of the old world. From the Stoic philosophers twenty centuries ago to the 19th Century Transcendentalists, we can be inspired with the eye-opening realization that "it is not what happens to us in life that affects us, but rather we are affected by our view of what happens."

We make our lives, by our view. We make our work by our vantage point of it.

The answer is simple. The transformation that passionate salon professionals are making is to re-look, from a higher view at the same old job, in the same old salon, with the same old clients, and same old teammates on the staff.

The message of the passionate salon professionals is that we have the ability to find a new vantage point, higher up the mountain where we can see more, hear more, feel more, love more and be more. We don't need to move our bodies to a new location. We just need to move our minds and hearts. Our bodies will follow. A haircutter who brings her hands to the salon has a job. The stylist who brings her hands and mind has a career. And the haircutter who brings her hands, mind and heart into the salon transforms herself into a passionate salon professional.

This book attempts to capture this transformation process from "cutting hair," to "changing the world." It is a process of becoming a true Renaissance stylist, who grows from not only knowledge in the science of cosmetology, but also is motivated by insights from the science of psychology. You will be learning about motivational psychology and will become just as much of a specialist in people as you are in hair, skin and nails. You will soon acquire knowledge and skills in three areas of motivational psychology; (1) self-motivation and coping with stressful salon situations, (2) the 10 passion skills to effectively relate to and be successful with your clients, (3) becoming a motivated, contributing team member.

You will find yourself becoming more whole as well. All of you, your hands, mind and heart will be taking the journey to become the passionate salon professional.

CHANGE YOUR LIFE TODAY!

The ideas in this book may change your life. We encourage you to become a PSP who looks at your contributions to your clients in more wholistic, more human ways, while, at the same time, offering them the best in technical skills. To view your work as one which both, cosmetically and psychologically, transforms the self-images and destinies of your fellow human beings in your chair.

Here is the only question you need to ask yourself to sense if you feel it inside to become part of the passionate salon professional movement:

"Do I just want to 'get by' in the salon?"
or
"Do I want to 'go for it,' and start changing the world, client by client?"

We never realize how important these special questioning moments are unless we, at some point, decide to "go for it." Later, we recall that defining moment as the one that changed our lives. If instead, we made the "get by" decision, chances are we didn't even notice the opportunity seed planted right here and now within our view.

Curiously we are always in these decision moments in our lives. In the salon these questions come to us in big, as well as in small, every day ways. These life changing passionate moments sometimes sound like this:

"I can feel it in my guts. I am going to become an expert in color. I will learn anything I can, travel to anywhere, I will learn everything I can about the best color techniques to be able to give every client more color in her life."

"Should I let our salon go on, as it is? Sure we are getting by and things are OK. But I dream of more that all of us can do together to make our salon world class for all of our clients. Why can't our clients experience us as the most caring salon professionals?"

"While still in beauty school, I attended my first hair show. The educators on the platform were open and non-intimidating and as I listened I realized there is so much more that I can do in this profession. Of course, I love working with clients in the salon, but I also could become a platform artist and this would keep me up to date, teach others, and be creative to help my clients back in my chair."

The ability to feel good inside, without anyone ever whispering an appreciative word, without a standing ovation, we suggest in this book, is the true answer to finding a personally passionate life, whether at work, or at home. Psychologists call this self-motivating style "intrinsic motivation."

Intrinsic motivation is the ultimate clue to a person's future success because the person's motivation is not dependent on outside, or extrinsic motivation factors. The drive comes from within and will always be there.

Or these life-changing moments can be experienced as simply as this:

"Should I sweep the hair off the floor which would involve me getting up and finding the broom, and all that? Yes, I have the opportunity now to make our beauty salon right here a more beautiful place where people can immediately feel cleaner, more respected, and just better."

"In my heart I know I can help my client Emily look so much better, but she just wants a cut. Should I just give her what she asked

for, or should I grow and get passionate about her new possibilities with my new professional products and services?

"Should I bring my personal problems into the salon dragging my teammates and my paying clients down, or should I take the higher road and decide to lift everyone else's day by focusing in on finding the good news in their lives?"

As a salon professional, you've had these moments. You, perhaps, are having one now. Do you want to choose the road to just "get by" or do you want to "go for it" and actualize all of your possibilities? If you are in beauty school, do you want to just go to school, or do you want to learn all you can to become your best? If you are in the salon, do you want to just go to work to make money to pay bills, or do you want to go into your same salon, with your same teammates and clients, owner and manager, and "go for it" and change the world?

Curiously your decision affects you, more than it affects anyone else. This moment is called a "transformational moment" because your decision can change your life. Your choice can give you purpose, rather than boredom. Your decision can turn your work life into your lifework.

You could say that your life depends on your answer. The by-product of these transformational moments is the energy called "passion." This book is about those who are choosing to make the high road decision to give them the fuel of passion to lift them up on to the higher, healthier and happier road of salon success.

THE ROOTS OF THE
PASSIONATE SALON PROFESSIONAL MOVEMENT

Hi, I'm Lew Losoncy (Dr. Lew). You might say I'm a Salon Psychologist. I fell in love with your profession in late seventies while working in my psychotherapy practice in Reading, Pennsylvania. Through one of my patients I found my way into your lifework. In my book with Donald Scoleri entitled, *The New Psy-cosmetologists: Blending the Sciences of Cosmetology and Psychology*, I wrote:

> *A dramatic experience provided the impetus for me to learn more about the professions of cosmetology and barber styling. Let me share with you the experience I had with one of my clients, Debbie, that caused such a change.*
>
> *Debbie was an attractive, 22 year-old woman whose major problem, shyness, kept her from reaching a goal of getting a date with a local accountant named David. Oh, understand, she knew his patterns, the local lounges he imbibed, and each Friday she would go to The Peanut Bar or R.J. Willoughby's to try to get close to the bespectacled bean counter, to no avail. He would totally ignore her and, frustrated, she would return to my "couch" to tell of her lack of progress with this "hunk." After hearing the same old song, week after week, I decided to encourage her to take a more assertive approach to fulfill her dreams of being with David.*
>
> *Maybe David himself is shy, Debbie. Perhaps he too would like to go out with you, but just doesn't know how to go about it. I have a thought. Why don't you initiate a conversation with him, and if you two seem to click, you can ask him out for dinner?*
>
> *What? You mean me just go right up to him, she shivered, and ask him out? A woman can't really do that, can she? I mean wouldn't that be too pushy?*
>
> *Well Deb, apparently what you are doing now isn't working, I replied. At worst, he'll ignore you, and that's exactly where you are*

now, isn't it? Imagine if you and David would really hit it off. No limits!

A thoughtful, anxious silence filled the room, and soon the petite blond lifted her chin with determination and replied, OK, Dr. Lew, I'm going to talk to David on Friday. I'm going to go right up and ask him out to dinner. That's that.

She left the office determined.

As our next appointment arrived, I wondered, did she or didn't she?

As she walked into the office I was surprised by her down demeanor. Instead of the enthusiastic Miss prancing into the room, in walked my client with a defeated, hang-dog expression. She slumped in her seat, and I had to ask her the big question.

Well, Deb, is there anything you'd like to tell me? I mean, did you ask David out on Friday?

Well, uh, no, she timidly responded.

Oh can you tell me why you didn't follow through on our plan?

She responded with three sentences that changed my life! Well, Doctor, I know you thought it would be a good idea to go up and talk to David. But, I talked to my hairdresser, and she thought it would be stupid. So I listened to her.

I was never the same again. Despite my years of schooling with a masters and doctorate in counseling psychology, Debbie trusted her hairdresser's advice about her personal problems over mine. (**The New Psy-cosmetologist, 4-5**)

How could her hairdresser gain such trust? You will learn why my patient listened and acted on her hairstylist's advice rather than her psychologists as you page through this book. I committed myself to discover everything I could about the stylist-client relationship from a psychologist's vantage point. For almost three decades I have been working full time with Matrix teaching the principles of Salon Psychology to salon professionals. It was there that I met Joe Santy, one of the most knowledgeable and caring salon owners and guest artists I ever experienced in my life. Joe has traveled the world helping salon professionals grow. This book grew out of the realization that a salon psychologist, coupled with a talented salon professional could offer insights on human behavior that could be practically applied to build "haircutters" into passionate salon professionals.

Hello! I'm Joe Santy. What a great profession we're in! Back in 1975, when I started in the beauty industry, I had no idea how helping others look and feel better about themselves could be so gratifying. On another level, elevating others elevated my own life to heights I am thankful to have reached. The secret is continuing your education both inside and outside the industry. Welcome to, and enjoy our passionate journey together!

YOUR PROFESSION HAS MANY PEOPLE TO THANK FOR ITS' PASSION AND MOTIVATION

Many inspiring, world changers have facilitated this transformational process in the worldwide beauty profession.

The initial breakthroughs in expanding the salon professional's self-image were instituted by the innovator and pioneer Douglas Cox. Doug brought and continues to bring the beauty profession to new levels of motivation and awareness about its potential. For many years, Doug has single-handedly taken the beauty profession up many challenging steps of pride.

Michael Cole employs humor and good business sense to keep the profession on solid ground with each step by offering "a little off the top," and numerous support materials.

Ann Mincey offers a spiritual growth emphasis, filled with wholistic themes to develop the whole person of the salon professional.

Geno Stempora's humor, delivered with charisma, complete his sound, passionate message. His passion for working behind the chair comes clearly through his animated lectures.

Donald Scoleri speaks from his heart, and everyone hears every beat.

Sharon Norman offers warmth, humor, inspiration, all with a very solid practical program to her fellow professionals.

Donn Matlack weaves words with wisdom in a deeply meaningful way.

Dennis Millard finds time as a salon owner to travel to teach salon professionals to think like owners.

The Zegarelli brothers, Arnold and Robert, their dedication to sharing practical and east-to-adapt techniques, and style forcasting trends imbued confidence and self-esteem to generations of stylists.

Tom Reid's soft style is heart warming and his ideas are practical and usable immediately.

Larry Curtis gets to the spiritual heart of salon success. Anyone who has ever met Larry knows he lives what he feels.

Many, many others have brought on this growth of the salon profession. In fact, today some salon owners and managers view staff motivation as a vital part of their training for their salon team.

In this book, we suggest that the passionate salon professionals learn Salon Psychology to make a transformation in their view of their work. That change involves moving from seeing oneself changing hair, skin and nails (things) to changing their client's lives (people) with their new motivating attitude and encouraging words. When you are finished reading this book and someone asks you what you do for a living, proudly reply, "I cosmetically and psychologically transform self-images and destinies of fellow human beings. I'm a passionate salon professional."

You will be experiencing the 10 processes to becoming a passionate salon professional. The word process reveals that the journey is an active, continuous one in which you are always in process, always proceeding to develop your passion for (1) your profession, (2) your clients and (3) your salon team or community.

Throughout the book we will be contrasting the attitudes, behaviors and the style of the "haircutter" versus a passionate salon professional (PSP). For purposes of this book, the term "haircutter" will refer to someone who looks at their career as just a job, while the passionate salon professional goes in each day to change the world."

PASSIONATE
SALON
PROFESSIONALS

TECHNICAL SKILLS + PASSION = THE PSP

1. PROFESSIONAL PASSION

2. CLIENT PASSION

3. TEAM PASSION

PASSIONATE SALON PROFESSIONALS
10 PROCESESS

PROFESSIONAL PASSION

Process I: "Move with a Higher Purpose"

Process II: "Bring Your Heart"

Process III: "Build Everything You Touch"

Process IV: "Be Driven from Within"

CLIENT PASSION

Process V: "Be Available"

Process VI: "Take Each Person One Step Higher"

TEAM PASSION

Process VII: "Discover Your Passionate Purpose Together"

Process VIII: "Value Your Community More than Your Ego"

Process IX: "Play with Reality"

Process X: "Find Your Way Together"

Contents

PASSIONATE SALON PROFESSIONALS

*"I cosmetically and psychologically transform
self-images and destinies of fellow human beings.
I'm a Passionate Salon Professional!"*

PART I: PROFESSIONAL PASSION

Process I: "Move with a Higher Purpose"

PART II: CLIENT PASSION

PART III: TEAM PASSION

PART

I

PROFESSIONAL PASSION

PROCESS I: "MOVE WITH A HIGHER PURPOSE"

PROCESS II: "BRING YOUR HEART"

PROCESS III: BUILD EVERYTHING YOU TOUCH"

PROCESS IV: BE DRIVEN FROM WITHIN"

 **PROCESS I**

"MOVE WITH A HIGHER PURPOSE"

The Haircutter	The Passionate Salon Professional
1. "I do hair."	1. "I touch my client physically and psychologically. I get closer to my clients than most professions. And touch builds trust"
2. "Who comes in comes in."	2. "I am with my clients through all the high and low times in their lives doing their hair for every major event in their lives"
3. "I'm not here to listen to her."	3. "I am one of the few people in my client's life who accepts her without any strings attached. No wonder she feels comfortable with me"
4. "I do her hair. I'm not paid to care about her."	4. "The look I recommend to my client is based on more than just her physical appearance. I take into consideration her self-image, personality and lifestyle"
5. "I do styling, coloring, perming."	5. "I find that people want color not for having color itself but rather because color will help them feel better about themselves"
6. "I go to work to pay bills."	6. "I go into the salon because I'm thrilled to help people look and feel great"

1

Interesting!
You Touch
Your Client's Hair, Skin,
Nails...
And Life!

*"All the beautiful sentiments in the world
weigh less than a single lovely action."*

—James Russell Lowell

The passionate salon professional doesn't take touching her client lightly. Elizabeth knew how important her touch was to her clients. She instructed her professional team, "The next time you touch your client's hair, skin or nails, be fully sensitive to the closeness you have with her, and how lucky you are to be able to build trust by making such close contact. Remember, your touch, and your close presence must be soothing and relaxing. And your touch may even serve to be healing of loneliness in this often cold, distant, impersonal world. Touch with the awareness that reveals you care, and you are safe."

YOU are in one of only five professions that have earned the privilege to touch their clients. You join the doctor, the dentist, nurse and massage therapist. You do what the lawyer, attorney, psychologist, accountant and engineer cannot do. You touch people. In fact you touch every one of your clients every day. And for some of your clients, you are the only one who touches him or her in their life.

And why is your touch so important?

Because your touch builds trust!

Touch is a vital need that you are fulfilling, especially in these times where everyone is more a number than a person, and relationships are most impersonal. Even the doctor-patient relationship has lost its warmth. The salon is one of those very few places left in today's world where human contact still has an opportunity for closeness. The more technology that exists in the world, the more people have a need for personal touch. There is no better place than your salon to fulfill one of the most basic of human needs, close contact with another. And this closeness is really highlighted through the smooth, soft touch of you, the caring, passionate salon professional.

Touch is so vital to humans that the noted psychologist Ashley Montagu wrote in Touching : "Touch is so important that it influences much of our thinking, even

NOTES

in our language. We speak of rubbing people the wrong way... a soft touch ... a smooth touch... we get in touch with other... we handle some people with kid gloves... some are thick or thin skinned... some get under our skin... others have to be handled with kid gloves, and still others are just touchy!"

Charles Panati, the scientific writer wrote in *Breakthroughs*, "We realize that human touch soothes, but it may also heal. In the future doctors and nurses may be trained to hold their patients' hands or stroke their patients' injuries."

The haircutter touches her client's hair; the passionate salon professional touches her client's life!

* * * *

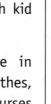

2

True!
You Are With Your
Client During Her Most
Emotional Times

*"No one is useless in the world
who lightens the burden of it on anyone else."*

—Charles Dickens

Carol had been through the years with her client Helen, 27 years in fact! She was privileged to perform the ceremonial "first styling," on Helen's one year-old, Susie. She gave Helen a full day total makeover for her and Ben's 30th Anniversary Party.

Helen was too sick to make it to the salon one Wednesday and Carol responded to her phone call and went to Helen's home where Helen received her weekly blow dry. One day later, an upset Ben called Carol in the salon to give her the tough news... and

NOTES

to thank her for being there on Wednesday, and for the past 27 years of Wednesdays for his loved one.

Carol was, maybe the last person to touch Helen as she gave her the final makeover. And the minister's eulogy included the reassuring thoughts that, "at least she was with her hairdresser Carol her final day."

YOU are with your clients anywhere from six to fifty-two times a year, and you see your clients more frequently then they see most of their relatives! You are with your clients during every emotional time in their life, every high and low, every birth and loss. And, you are touching them. No wonder they feel close to you. You are designing their appearance for every major event in their lives. You prepare them for their first day of pre-school, their entry into kindergarten, their high school prom and their high school picture. When you think of it, their picture in their high school yearbook is highlighted with your artistry, and will live for years and years.

You could say that your work will live on forever!

How could you not be passionate about what you do?

You hear everything going on in your clients' lives, don't you?

"Guess what, I can count"

"I got a puppy"

"I won the spelling bee"

"I made the cheer leading squad"

"I didn't get accepted to State"

"My boyfriend said he didn't want to see me anymore"

"I met this great guy in college"

"He asked me to marry him"

"Will you do my hair for my wedding"

"This is little Gabbie"

"Gabbie starts school tomorrow!"

You are there, with your client, during every high and low. And you are touching her life. How could you not be passionate about your work?

* * * *

3

Hmm!
You Accept Your Client
Unconditionally
(And You May Be The
Only One)

*"I have made a conscious effort not to ridicule,
not to belittle, not to scorn human actions, but
to understand them."*

—Baruch Spinoza

The unconditional acceptance by passion-ate salon professionals creates a secure environment for long-term relationships to evolve. The old adage that "only your hairdresser knows," is validation of this concept of unconditional acceptance.

Sharon, who had always been shy, had a hard time as an adult making friends. Because of her aloofness, most people thought that she was stuck up, snobby or

NOTES

had a superiority complex. Jim, her stylist for the last eight years, knew differently after meeting Sharon. In that close relationship filled with touch and unconditional acceptance, Sharon began feeling more comfortable and confident with Jim. Sharon started opening up to Jim discussing more and more about new looks and meeting new people. Jim saw these changes, and over a period of time, started noticing that Sharon was not only growing in the salon, but in the outside world. Without his unconditional acceptance of Sharon, right from that first meeting, She may have never overcome her shyness problem, experiencing all of the gifts she had to give to the world, and what life could offer her.

YOU not only touch your client's life during all of her emotional times, but you have another special opportunity to build a close relationship with your client. You accept her. With no strings attached.

Psychologist Carl Rogers argued that ideal, wholesome relationships have elements of "unconditional acceptance" in them. Unconditional acceptance is present in a relationship when one person is not judging another person's words or actions and accepts the other as she honestly describes her life. Obviously when we are in a relationship with unconditional acceptance, we feel safe, comfortable and we open up to the other. These relationships are very therapeutic, but they are very, very rare. How many people do you have in your life who accept you, don't judge you, and truly listen to you without telling you what to do? If you have one, you are very, very lucky.

A good stylist-client relationship comes closer to an unconditional relationship than most other professional relationships. The teacher evaluates you when grading your papers, a parent demands certain behaviors, a doctor gives advice and even the minister, priest and rabbi often shepherd their members in one direction or another. But the passionate salon professional just listens with empathy, warmth and respect.

Considering you touch your client, you are with her during every emotional event in her life and you unconditionally accept her, you can understand why my (Dr. Lew) patient Debbie trusted her stylist more than me!

*   *   *   *

NOTES

4

Yes!
You Have The
Professional Skills and
Tools to Design Your
Client's Image of
Herself

*"There is a loftier ambition than merely to
stand high in the world.
It is to stoop down and lift mankind
a little higher."*

—Henry Van Dyke

A mental "wow!" exploded in Mike's mind as a smile of satisfaction filled up his proud face. His client, Chantele, a young beautiful, financial secure woman just finished praising the young stylist for his creative work: an ego stroke of the highest caliber backed with sincerity!

NOTES

Mike, a stylist of three years had pondered in beauty school what single aspect of beauty he could specialize in to make his work stand out in the minds of every person who sits in his hair. Armed with the answer to the question "Why do clients change stylists?" Mike knew the number one reason was because, "the client felt she always looked the same." So Mike decided to become a passionate salon professional who was a change specialist.

In a naïve way, Mike didn't realize that by going to shows, watching DVD's, attending an advanced academy once a year and always having the latest in styling tools and technology, it would give him a tremendous advantage over other stylists. When a stylist keeps updating her skills and technology, the client's expectations are heightened about what benefits this passionate salon professional has to offer. A stagnant stylist can't compete with this treatment.

Mike always took the compliments Mrs. Smith gave him for granted. After all, she was overweight. And Shelley's praise for Mike's work fell on the stylist's deaf ears, because, as she describes herself, "not as pretty as others in her class." Mr. Long with a few dozen hairs, felt like a million when Mike was finished with him.

Mike's "aha" today, and the key to his smile was that because of his skill training and learning the latest tools all of his clients received a lift based on their style. Not just the people that Mike thought needed it anyway.

Mike realized at the moment of Chantele's praises, what kind of power his skills wielded. He helped all clients to stand taller, act more confidently, and have a better self-image solely based on their hairstyle.

YOU design your client's image of herself. Through your special relationship involving your touch, your presence with her during all of her life experiences, and your unconditional acceptance, you earn the right to learn about her lifestyle and dreams. And then you have the professional artistry, skills and tools to design her image to look great. Think about it. You can create a sexy look, a professional look, a classic look, a conservative or attention getting look, a look to wear for a college admissions interview, a prom or wedding look, and even a look for the suspect to clean up his act for the jury!

The image that you, as a passionate salon professional can create influences a person in least four ways.

1. Our image of ourselves is revealed in *our physical appearance*. Our range of appearance from worst to best can be dramatically influenced by the artistry of a passionate salon professional.

2. Our image influences *our psychological self*. This will be detailed in the next section.

3. Our image affects *our social appearance*. How we look is what people first see. Our first impression that we give to people is our physical appearance. Our hairstyle, color and makeup tell a story that the

NOTES

other person consciously or non-consciously experiences.

4. Our image affects *our academic and professional success*. Research is clear that students who are better groomed get better grades in school. Its wrong, but its a fact. Research also reveals that better-groomed real estate agents earn more money. When we look like we are "together," we are given a different treatment because of the respect that our image commands. Again, we don't think this is right, but it is a fact.

Why wouldn't your client want all of these advantages? A salon that only focuses on the new look for a client to have a physical beneficial lift, is underselling what it has to offer. Get passionate. Give your clients all of the benefits that new look can give them.

Then ask yourself how much your service now is really worth!

* * * *

5

Wow!
You Affect Your Client's Total Self, Not Just Her Hair, But Her Levels of Courage, Confidence and Hope

"Self-confidence is the first requisite to great undertakings."

—Samuel Johnson

Have you ever had a bad hair day or a bad haircut? Of course you have, everyone has. What did it feel like? Now contrast that with a great hair day. You walked taller, felt better, even invincible!

Chuck's wiry, coarse hair betrayed him. When he was younger the other kids taunted him — Mr. Brillo Pad, Spring Head and the list goes on. As an adult he

NOTES

was reserved, shy and embarrassed; especially when a girl caught his eye, because of his hair. He jumped from stylist to stylist for twenty-six years, never once being satisfied with his hair. Chuck's styles took in everything from reverse perms to relaxers, and every imaginable type of cut. Unfortunately, nothing seemed to work for the sad client.

One Saturday drive, Chuck spotted a salon's "Grand Opening," sign and decided to give it a try. After all, what did he have to lose, since his hair has never looked good? A bouncy, petite stylist named Jeanette greeted him. The clear-faced stylist actively listened as twenty-six years of bad hair days poured out of Chuck's heart. Always up on the latest chemical technologies, Jeanette suggested a new service that smoothes curly hair and helps to make it controllable. Chuck took in Jeanette's confidence and decided to give it a try.

When Jeanette was finished styling Chuck's hair, she turned him towards the mirror, his eyes widened he took in a deep breadth and exclaimed, "That looks great! For the first time my hair looks like hair!"

Six weeks later Chuck was back in Jeanette's chair for a trim along with his newfound confidence. Jeanette was introduced to Chuck's newfound girlfriend, June, who was to become Jeanette's newfound client!

YOU can look at what you do as styling hair or styling peoples' lives. You can view your work as adding color to a client's hair, but aren't you really adding color to their life? People are whole beings, and when you influence any part of them, you are influencing them. When they look good, they feel better. Hair isn't something on their head, hair is *them*. When your client's hair is unmanageable, they experience their life as unmanageable.

When you change a person's psychological image of her self, her self-image, she acts differently in life. Her attitude changes and her behavior changes. She may go out to the party the night you do her hair, and she might have stayed home if you didn't.

Our self-image is who we perceive ourselves to be. The world-renowned plastic surgeon Maxwell Maltz wrote in *Psycho-cybernetics*, "The self-image is the key to the personality and human behavior. Change the self-image and you change the personality and the behavior. More than this the self-image sets the boundaries of individual achievement. It defines what you can and cannot do. Expand the self-image and you expand the area of the possible. The development of an adequate, realistic self-image seems to imbue the individual with new capabilities and new talents. It literally turns failure into success."

As a passionate salon professional you can change your client's self-image, both physically and psychologically.

*   *   *   *

6

Why Not?
You Can Transform
Your Tough Worklife
Into Your Lifework

*"When love and skill work together,
expect a masterpiece."*

—John Ruskin

Tony goes to the salon with nothing to look forward to than a day of mechanical haircuts. His attitude doesn't allow him to hear compliments any more because his thinking is one of, "its just a job." Tony's days appear long, and by day's end he is burned out and exhausted. Tony has a "work life."

Mary goes to the salon, upbeat and positive, realizing her skills, both technical and people, are helping her clients feel better about themselves. Her beauty career has fulfilled her lifelong passion of helping

NOTES

people look better on the outside, and feel better on the inside. She is constantly taking courses in beauty while developing her customer service skills to fulfill her passionate purpose. Mary's days are not only meaningful and fun, but by the end of the day, Mary is elated at what she has accomplished with clients in her lifework making people feel and look great.

Curiously, both Tony and Mary work in the same salon.

YOU can go to work, to make money, to pay bills or you can go in to the salon with the purpose of cosmetically and psychologically transforming the self-image and destinies of fellow human beings. In the song "*Hey Jude*" the Beatles sang: "all the movement that you need is on your shoulder." What we need is not a new outside life, but a new view of our everyday life. By looking at your work differently, you can turn your work life into your lifework. If you do, you'll never have to go to work again. You can go in to change the world.

In *The New Psy-Cosmetologists*, Donald Scoleri and Dr. Lew Losoncy wrote, "In the United States and Canada alone, about 200,000 salons are influencing the appearance of 26 million humans a week. And in some cases, it goes even further than that. Could it be that these 26 million people are actually even feeling better about themselves and their lives? Could it be that these clients are gaining a little more courage, confidence and hope during this magical half hour?"

NOTES

"What other profession in the world could make a claim of touching people on a regular basis for a period of years while giving the life-changing gifts of beauty and confidence? Doesn't it give you a permanent lift knowing that you are part of this network of life-changers?"

The "Silent Angels" in a Wisconsin salon make notes of needy people, sometimes their client, sometimes families their clients talk about and during the holidays drop off gifts for the children, without even taking credit. Thousand of salons do cut-a-thons each year to benefit local causes. And the greatest benefits are experienced in the hearts of the passionate givers.

Feel the passion for influencing the world, client by client. Change your work life into your lifework.

* * * *

 PROCESS II

"BRING YOUR HEART"

The Haircutter	The Passionate Salon Professional
7. "I'm still mad at what happened last week in the salon."	7. "The past is past, its over. That's why its called the past."
8. "I'm worried about how busy we are going to be during the holidays. How will we handle it?"	8. "Now is my only moment in which I have any control. So I'm living now."
9. "I don't need to learn any new services. I'm doing OK."	9. "A year from now I want to be not only a great stylist, but great at perming and great at retailing."
10. "Someday I'll see how much I can do in one day."	10. "Today is going to be the biggest volume day of my life."
11. "Most of my customers just want a trim so that's what I give them."	11. "Today I'm going to try new approaches to helping my clients look their best."
12. "Haircutting is just a job."	12. "I am going to get myself pumped up when I am with each of my clients today."

7

Get Over Yesterday, Before It Gets Over You

*"The past is past.
That's why its called, 'the past'".*

The accolades never seemed to stop for Nick on his graduation day from State Cosmetology College. His teachers and fellow students kept telling him what a great stylist he was and what an awesome future he has in the profession. That day was, unfortunately, his finest moment. He lived that day, not only that day, but still re-lives that day over and over again every day. Nick felt that any salon should be honored to have somebody of his stature on the staff. Interviews with Nick quickly revealed that his only achievements were over. Despite that, a salon in a Northeastern US city, with a good reputation took a chance and hired. Nick reluctantly agreed to their

NOTES

training program, even though he thought he should have taught it!

On the first day of training he allowed his attitude to get in the way. While being shown a system for precision haircutting, he argued that he could get the same result a different way (he couldn't). His first week on the floor produced a number of client complaints to which Nick responded, "I am a good hairdresser. If there is a problem between us, it must be you." Needless to say, Nick is now selling cars.

Nick never got over his past, so his past got over him. One final question: What does a great past and a terrible past have in common? They are both over.

YOU can be an archeologist and keep digging up your past. Or you can be an architect and use today to build your future. Which will work better?

Think about your past this way: You played golf yesterday and came in with a round of 150. As you walk up to the first tee today, take a look at your new scorecard. Nothing but your name is written on it. Don't carry yesterday's score with you today because you will be writing new numbers on your scorecard today. Today offers a new game.

If you have had a difficult past, or even a horrible day yesterday in the salon, reassure yourself with a laugh by telling yourself, "My past is over. That's why its called the past. My past is a myth and a fiction today. Today will be whatever I will make it. I have a new scorecard and new opportunities now!"

There at least three reasons to get over your past.

1) When you focus in on your past, you are using your power in this important now moment dwelling on what was, rather than what could be. You are re-living, rather than living. How many moments of your potential are lost because of wasting your time on what was?

2) A second problem with re-living your past is that it not only consumes this power moment of now, but it gives you very little accurate information. How can you ever know for sure that you are afraid of selling or public speaking today because of this or that experience in your past?

3) The third problem with digging up your past is that you start finding more and more things to blame to get angry about. You dig an even deeper depressing hole for yourself.

Get over it now! When your attitude today dwells on reliving your yesterdays, you lose all of your potential power right in front of you now. Get over those resentments from yesterday. When someone tells you she has had a difficult past, look at her and empathetically respond, "I'm sorry to hear that. But I have great news for you. Its over now!"

* * * *

8

Today Is Your Best Chance To Change Your Life

"Now is your only moment of power."

Judy's personal life has been rocky for a few tough months. She can't seem to get out of her slump. Her first Tuesday morning client, Allison, reveals to Judy that her sister's fourteen-year-old son was just diagnosed with inoperable brain cancer. Judy pauses, and listens to her young client reflect on life.

As Allison looks directly at Judy, she shares that, in the end, the gift of today is all we really have, isn't it? If we have today, we always have a chance to keep our dreams moving and alive. After Allison leaves, Judy realizes that she has many, many choices in her life. She has much to be grateful for, her health, a profession she loves, and caring clients. While Judy was still deeply concerned about her client's nephew, Allison's words enlightened Judy to the power of the moment.

NOTES

Instead of waiting for life to reach out to her and give her meaning, Judy reached inside of herself realizing she is the only one who can pull her out of the slump. And that taking advantage of the power of today is all she really needs!

YOU are alive! And being alive gives you some options, doesn't it? Three of your options include going into the salon, doing your job and getting by. Your other option is to create within you a sense of urgency. In that sense of urgency, to really make something out of your work and your life you realize, "I must get started today, because today is the best chance to change my life!"

Saying you'll start tomorrow is easy but ineffective because your actions of tomorrow are not coming with your commitment today. Tomorrow is always easier to quit smoking and start exercising, isn't it?

You have about two and a half billion seconds of life. But only one of these moments count. This moment called now. Today is the best day to change your life.

Who are you in the process of becoming? Take some time to create your new self. And then on the next idea you'll have a discussion with your older, wiser self to adjust your goals.

1) **Your Physical Self:** What is your ideal goal for your physical self? Who are you in the process of becoming physically, beginning now. How will you look in a week? Month? Year? How much will you weigh in

a month? How could you make yourself healthier through diet and exercise? Feel it happening already! You are now in process!

2) **Your Social Self:** Who are you in the process of becoming socially? Can you see yourself as more outgoing, or more assertive, or more tolerant of others? Identify some social goals you have for yourself that are happening at the moment you are imagining them happening.

3) **Your Professional Self:** Who are you in the process of becoming in your salon? What could you do more of, or become better at in your salon? What new skills could you learn? Are you in the process of becoming a better retailing expert? Perming? Coloring? Skin Care? Manicuring? Pedicuring?

4) **Your Financial Self:** How much did you earn last year? How much will you earn this year? How could you give yourself a raise and earn more per client? How could you get more clients off of your current clients? Imagine yourself now in the process of earning more money than you have ever earned in your life.

5) **Your Spiritual Self:** Who are you in the process of becoming spiritually? In what ways would you like to become a better person? Experience yourself in the process of becoming a better you.

6) Now make a list of 100 things you are going to do or experience or learn in your life. Force yourself to do this list because if you do, within a week you will check off a few and during your lifetime, you

NOTES

will check off many. But if you don't have a list, your life will be up to the way the winds blow.

100 Things You are Going to Do, to Experience & Learn in Your Life

1. _____

2. _____

3. _____

4. _____

5. _____

6. _____

7. _____

8. _____

9. _____

10. _____

11. _____

12. _____

13. _____

14. _____

15. _____

16. _____

17. _____

18._____

19._____

20._____

21._____

22._____

23._____

24._____

25._____

26._____

27._____

28._____

29._____

30._____

31._____

32._____

33._____

34._____

35._____

36._____

37._____

38._____

NOTES

NOTES

39._____

40._____

41._____

42._____

43._____

44._____

45._____

46._____

47._____

48._____

49._____

50._____

51._____

52._____

53._____

54._____

55._____

56._____

57._____

58._____

59._____

60._____

61._____

62._____

63._____

64._____

65._____

66._____

67._____

68._____

69._____

70._____

71._____

72._____

73._____

74._____

75._____

76._____

77._____

78._____

79._____

80._____

NOTES

NOTES

81._____

82._____

83._____

84._____

85._____

86._____

87._____

88._____

89._____

90._____

91._____

92._____

93._____

94._____

95._____

96._____

97._____

98._____

99._____

100._____

Today Is The Best Chance To Change Your Life!

9

Have A Talk With Your Older, Wiser Self About Who She Wants You To Be In Five Years

*"What does your last decision tell you about
who you are in
the process of becoming?"*

—Lew Losoncy

Judy, in the previous example, left the salon that day with a new view. She felt bad about her client's nephew; however, it helped to signal a shift in attitude for her. She pondered on what would be the best avenue to get her professional and personal life back on track. The determined stylist decided to find a tranquil area by the stream in the nearby shady park and imagine what life would be like for her in a few years. She imagined she was five years older. Remembering an exercise she had learned at a seminar a few years back, Judy

NOTES

put her thoughts into writing as if five years had already passed. She imagined being older, wiser and wrote about her personal and professional life in detail; starting five years out, and bringing it back to the present.

The complete transformational experience took Judy only about ninety minutes. And the magical change appeared throughout her body. Judy started breathing deeper, a beautiful smile warmed her face, and her posture was clearly more defined, as her step was higher than it had been for months. Judy was in the process of becoming her dream.

YOU have a real wise person inside you. One who has more wisdom than you do today. You have your older, wiser self. Say to her, "Let's talk."

Imagine yourself five years from now. How old will you be? How might you look? What kind of attitude might you have? Will you be married? Where will you live? What kind of a car will you drive? How much will you be earning per year? What kind of professional services will you be an expert at? Now picture yourself five years older and ask yourself a few questions and let your older, wiser self-answer.

Question 1. "Older, wiser self, what is the single most important thing I should do today so that when I become you, I will be happy I made that decision?"

Question 2. "Older, wiser self, what should I become better at in our salon so that I can earn more and be even better at helping my clients look their best?"

Question 3. "Older, wiser self, what habits can I change and what can I do to be as healthy and in-shape person so that when I become you, I am even better than I am today."

Question 4. "Older, wiser self, what should I do about a current challenge, problem, conflict, crises or struggle so that it is resolved long before I grow into you?"

Older, wiser self, thank you for the direction you gave me. Actually, I'll be you in a few years.

* * * *

10

Do The Things You Hate To Do First

'Start by doing what's necessary, than what is possible and suddenly you are doing the impossible."

—St. Francis of Assissi

NOTES

A major part of the beauty profession and one that is oft times overlooked is the cleanliness of the area where you work and spend a third of your life. Many clients will change salons over cleanliness before they will over price!

You know that upset tone of someone's voice? The whole staff could hear it in Stefanie's words. They could see it in the contortions of her face, and clenched fists and just know that the prima donna was being reminded again to clean her mirrors, the back and base of her chair, and sanitize her tools. She snubbed her nose at cleaning because, as a "stylist," this demeaning task was beneath someone like her.

NOTES

Passionate salon professionals take pride in their work and in creating uplifting, clean, sanitized surroundings. Joanne crisply arrives at the salon well before her first scheduled appointment. She insists she needs time to check her station and prepare herself for the day. The enthusiastic redhead knows that it is everyone's job to keep the salon spotless because a dissatisfied client is a reflection on the whole salon, and not just a particular stylist. Doing the things you hate to do first gives you a feeling of self-control, accomplishment and makes the rest of your day more fulfilling. And anyway, wasn't the original name, a "beauty" salon!

YOU sit around your house on Sunday morning and its a mess. Looking at the sloppy table with all of the dirty glasses, you realize that the dishwasher is full and you can't put the dishes in it. And the floors are crusty. And that's just one room! You feel depressed. This afternoon you are going to clean this mess up. Right now, you are going to get some coffee and may do some shopping. You're not really enjoying your cup of coffee because that sightless apartment keeps appearing in your head.

There is an answer. Do it now. Get it done. Get momentum on your side. Move quickly. A huge project isn't huge. Its just a bunch of small projects. A seven-course dinner is simple, one course seven times. Building a house isn't a big project. Its just a series of one board and one brick at a time.

So, take out that first clean dish in the dishwasher and put it away. Now the second one and more. Put the dirty ones in the dishwasher and turn it on. Now get the vacuum out and dance it over the floor. Get it started now. Soon you are living in a great looking spotless place. Stay home, make your own coffee and sit down and listen to your favorite music. Relax. You now have a clean mind and a clean house. You feel great.

Remember, do the things you don't like to do first. If you don't, then you have to do them over and over again in your mind a thousand times. And, in the end, you still have to do them anyway, don't you?

What responsibility in the salon do you dislike the most? Do those jobs first. And then your mind is free to do what you enjoy.

*   *   *   *

NOTES

11

Develop An Appreciation For Your Life!

"Self-knowledge is the beginning of self-improvement."

—Spanish proverb

The beauty industry affords an excellent opportunity for stylists to appreciate their lives as they learn about the lives of others. Mitch always had an interest in the occupations and income levels of his clients; however, his interest was far from noble. Instead of being thankful for his job and income level, he used his gathered information to fuel the fires of back room gossip in the salon. "Look what Susan makes as a nurse." "Sean is an architect and he makes a fortune." "We work too hard in here for too little money." Mitch, even surrounded by the diversity of the clients he has, doesn't appreciate that there will always be

NOTES

those better off, and more times than not, people less fortunate.

Doris works with Mitch and attempts to neutralize any negativity that Mitch spews. She tells the other stylists that the more you can learn about others, the larger the pool of information you have to pull from for your own life. As far as finances and money goes "If someone's grass looks greener, find out what fertilizer they're using." Go for the positive. Don't turn their green grass into crab grass with your negativity. Doris knows it is the love of the profession first, and has found the financial benefits will automatically follow. Doris's view gives her entry into the PSP network!

Being a passionate salon professional gives you a heartfelt gratitude for your own life as you connect with the lives of so many different others.

YOU are literally a miracle! You are such a rare combination of the physical and spiritual that there is no one anywhere in the world, exactly like you. You are the owner of your body, your mind, your actions, thoughts, feelings and your attitude. Even your dreams are uniquely yours. And this is your moment in the history of our magnificent universe. You are alive and this gives you the power to draw up the blueprint for your life experiences.

Passionate salon professionals are lovers and appreciators of their lives. They love people and are curious about what makes people tick. They crave new experi-

ences in life and even find new exciting ways of viewing that same old client in their chair after a decade. Curiously, passionate salon professionals often do not frequently associate with people from their profession outside of the salon. They find that when they are always with the same people they work with, they start grinding through the daytime problems over and over again, even at night. They have friends from all walks of life to get a rich social mixture and to stay out of the rut of sameness.

And passionate salon professionals love reading books that keep them motivated. They clearly prefer positive and meaningful books that can change their life. As one Virginia stylist concluded, "How can reading about the love life and divorce of a soap opera star enrich my life to the same degree as a good book or poem?" curiously, they often will re-route gossip, or excuse themselves walking away to do some thing more meaningful for them. And the easiest way of recognizing a passionate salon professional is her constantly refreshing new looks in hair and clothing.

To develop a further appreciation for life, feel a sense of gratitude for all of the things that you do have, rather than resentment for all of the things that you don't have. Generate your ability to feel in awe of life, of nature, of children and of your salon's possibilities to give your clients and your team a better life.

* * * *

12

Start Yourself "Flowing" Into Happiness

"Do what you want to do... But want to do what you are doing. Be what you want to be...But want to be what you are."

"Permanent waving-what a drag!! It's rote, it's boring, it's, it's a pain in the neck!"

So says, JoJo, a frustrated California stylist, as she ranted on and on to me (Joe Santy) on the show floor at the I.C.E. Show in Los Angeles. The rest of the members of her team echoed the blonde stylist's feelings. All the stylists in her salon avidly avoided perms; however, JoJo had the vision that to be a well rounded professional, perming was an essential skill she needed to acquire.

I explained to the open-minded stylist that the more details you learn about any service, including perming and coloring, the more you're able to see and approach your work in new ways. You open up opportunities where none existed before.

NOTES

JoJo's eyes widened when I shared three ideas on the power of mastering texture. Her first texture eye-opener was to discover that a full perm could be done using twelve rods.

She responded, "No way!" when she learned that there were at least thirty-two different ways of wrapping a perm. Her third insight arrived to her when we observed that almost every client walking on the busy show floor could use some type of texture service. Being a self-starter, JoJo vowed to give perming a try with a new attitude.

Three years later, at the same California event, an exuberant JoJo jumped onto the stage after our first show. Her thankful hug suggested she had something important to tell me. The animated JoJo proudly relayed to me her permanent waving triumph! She had researched and experimented with different types of perming techniques and lotions. What she found was that once she mastered the wraps, felt at ease choosing the right lotion and was clear in communicating the right knowledge to the client, the perms literally sold themselves! Now when a client comes in for a perm JoJo says she is able to get into it with such an intense passion that time just flies. She found that by increasing her knowledge about texture, her understanding deepened, making perming as easy as breathing. Her new perspective allowed her to experience the wonderful state of "flow!"

YOU are flowing when you are so immersed or so "into" an experience that you are unaware of time, or anything else going on in the outside world. When flowing you aren't self-consciously thinking, "Am I doing OK?" Your mind isn't wandering because you are totally there. Many psychologists believe that when we are flowing we are in the ultimate transcendent state of happiness. And the most interesting and exciting fact about flowing is that research indicates that we can bring it on, whenever we choose.

NOTES

HOW DO YOU GET YOURSELF INTO A FLOW STATE?

1) Start taking every experience and imagine you are using a magnifying glass to see and experience more of what you are observing. As you make the experience larger, begin to see more, finding details that you previously overlooked. In studying your client, notice each strand of hair or each facial blemish.

2) Now hear more. If a client is talking, make her words louder and fuller. Give her words more meaning.

3) Feel more. Experience your relationship with your client more fully.

4) Creating changes. Begin looking at the details in your client's appearance that you can see yourself improving. Imagine how you would proceed. Experience your client's looks as being in the process of changing and becoming better and better through your artistry.

5) Let yourself go. Let yourself flow. Feel the process as it is happening. Get into the picture. Experience

NOTES

yourself as both in the picture and an observer of the picture.

When we are flowing, we are not living today for something that we will get tomorrow. Flow moments are not means to ends, but are ends in themselves. A passionate salon professional does not recommend a total makeover on Tuesday because of a reward, a bigger paycheck on Friday. The reward comes now, in the state of flow on Tuesday. This way the passionate salon professional has rewarding moments every day, not once every fourteen days at paycheck time. In Beauty School a student in flow doesn't go to class today to study science for the test next week, but rather goes to class today to learn new ideas to feel great today.

Flowing involves arranging the contents of your conscious mind to find meaning in whatever you are doing in this moment. No one can put you into flow. And no one can stop you from flowing. The ability to create flow is the self-starter's ability to create personal happiness. Happiness is available anytime, anyplace, even in cleaning the floor or washing the windows. The higher view is seeing yourself in the process of building a cleaner world.

* * * *

 # PROCESS III

"BUILD EVERYTHING YOU TOUCH"

The "Haircutter"	The Passionate Salon Professional
13. "She makes me angry."	13. "Nobody is powerful enough to make me angry unless I let them."
14. "I'm no good at retailing. I tried and the client didn't want any. I'm just afraid."	14. "I am determined to master recommending professional products. My clients need them and each time I recommend one I get better."
15. "I can't stand my two o'clock."	15. "I change the way I look at difficult customers by imagining there is one simple fact I am missing about her, that if I knew it I would understand her."
16. "I hate these changes."	16. "Let's learn this new computer. In a short while, we will have learned better ways of serving our clients."

13

Whatever You Blame You Give Your Power Away To

"Everything that irritates us about others can lead us to an understanding of ourselves."

—Carl Jung

"Mrs. Drew hates her color. I just can't satisfy her." I am working twenty hours a week. How come I'm not making a lot of money? I guess I am just a lousy hairdresser"

These are the lamentations of Lynn, a stylist of a dozen years. Instead of approaching each challenge individually and coming to a powerful solution for each client, she chose the negative way out. Blaming the clients for not knowing what they wanted, badmouthing the beauty industry and even confiding in the salon owner that it was probably time to quit the business. All nonsense! By giving up her power she bought into her own emotional insecurities.

NOTES

Nancy, on the other hand, has also been a stylist for twelve years. The perky thirty something beauty artist has the same challenges with short and long term clients. She knows the "power" is being able to satisfy her clients. Her "power" starts with a good consultation, a clear understanding of what the client wants, Nancy takes the responsibility communicating back to the client what the service will entail, especially the end result. Nancy is convinced that ninety percent of service errors can be avoided with a good consultation. Service challenges, which include wrong color, perm too tight, straightening reverted, and more are accepted by Nancy confidently and with full accountability, even when she wasn't at fault.

She appreciates every client, knowing that her clients pass numerous salons to get to hers. Her "power" comes in her choosing to neutralize the clients' anxiety/anger over the situation, and simply correct the problem. Blame has no place in Nancy's vocabulary.

YOU may have said to yourself at times something like "Mrs. Jones makes me mad." And indeed you are angry at her for causing you to be upset. But, your anger was not caused directly by Mrs. Jones, but rather by what you are telling yourself about Mrs. Jones.

Here's proof. If Mrs. Jones did the same thing to 1000 stylists, would all 1000 be angry? Certainly not. Some would have been angry also, of course. Others would have tried to understand why Mrs. Jones did what she did. Was she having a bad day? Was she disappointed in the style I gave her? Was she acting like that because she was waiting too long? Still other stylist might have thought, "I wonder how I can turn Mrs. Jones' attitude around and get her laughing." And still others might have gone the other way and thought, "I'd love to grab that woman and shake her!"

The fact is that we are not affected by what happens to us, but rather by what we tell ourselves about what happened to us. So when you listen to stylists who are unhappy, angry, hurt or experiencing upset emotions the one common thing you will hear is that they are blaming something for causing their unhappiness. In other words, they are making the cause of their unhappiness someone or something else. And, by doing that, they are giving their emotional power away to whatever they are choosing to blame.

Look at it this way:

The Outside Stimulus	causes	My Blaming Response
Client didn't like my cut	and . . .	"I felt angry at her and hurt"

The haircutter believes the outside experiences cause her inside feelings. But, the passionate salon professional avoids blaming the outside world for the way she is feeling, and instead of blaming the outside world, takes the same event and builds her inside view of the outside experience. Sense this reaction to the same experience:

The Outside Stimulus	My View of the Experience	My Response
"Client didn't like my cut."	"I'll thank her for telling me what she didn't like and give her a look she likes."	"I'll create a look that will satisfy her her needs and will keep her as a client."

The passionate salon professional is determined to stop blaming others in the outside world and giving their power away — and instead, to start building their inside world. Remember that it's not what happens to you in life that affects you, but rather it's the way you look at what happens to you that does.

* * * *

14

Make Your Passion For Trying New Things Stronger Than Your Fear Of Failing

"Adversity cause some people to break and others to break records."

—William A. Ward

Betsy calmly pages through the appointment book until... until the word "Foil Highlighting" brings her fears to her face! Her hands become clammy, she starts sweating, and her stomach twists and churns as she faces the fact that her first client next Friday morning wants foils. And that's only five days away! Her thinking continues, "I could get sick on Friday, but that's my big book day, or maybe I could just quit!"

Oh, the beauty school she attended did touch on foils; however, in the school's clinic, frosting caps were the tool of choice. A voice inside Betsy's head made it perfectly clear that her reaction to seeing the foil highlighting on Friday was an overreaction. In addition to her exposure to foils in beauty school, she had seen the process performed at distributor shows and at her salon where she noticed other stylists making a ton of money mastering foils.

Curiously, Betsy was always the first one of her friends to try new things outside of the industry. The staff and all of her clients still talk about her Montana skydiving, State Fair bungee jumping, and Colorado white water rafting. The same girl is frightened by foils!

Betsy decided she would turn up the heat on her comfort level, invited their manicurist Monica to be her foiling model on Monday night. The young stylist grabbed her tail comb and foils, determined to conquer her unwarranted fears. Monica was thrilled with her color and talked about her foils with her nail clients. The session paid off in building Betsy's foiling finesse. Curiously, she realized that her passion for trying new things outside the industry became the catalyst for overcoming her fears within the industry. Monica would love Betsy to foil her again, but just never skydive!

YOU see a new style at your professional distributor's hair show and you love it! But it looks so complicated. And this world famous guest artist has golden hands. And you know you could never do that style, but you just love it. And you go back to your salon and talk about it with the other stylists and you tell some of your clients about it, but you never try it because you believe you could never do anything that good.

Was there a time you weren't potty trained? We bet! What if you would have said to yourself then, "I'll guess I'll never be potty trained because I'm not potty trained now!" Was there a time you couldn't read nor write, nor color, nor perm? What if you would have told yourself, "These things are too hard. I know I'll never be able to read or write or color or perm!"

If so, today, you wouldn't be coloring, perming, reading or writing, and sadly, not potty trained!

Every moment of growth involves developing the passion to learn something new, something that you can use for the rest of your life. Make your passion to learn new things in the salon stronger than your fear of failing. Start off by developing the courage to be imperfect, the courage to act without guarantees. The courage to know that the first time you try something it won't be perfect, but the second time you try it, it will be better. And if you keep trying it you'll become great. Keep on and you will master it. And do it more and maybe you will become... that world famous guest artist on stage! Not necessarily because she was better than you. Probably because, she made her passion for trying new things stronger than her fear of failing!

NOTES

* * * *

15

Use Your Thought Bricks To Build Rather Than To Destroy

"You become what you think about"

—Napoleon Hill

Rich, a stylist for two years has reached a point where he wondered if the beauty industry was right for him. He loves his work but building a clientele has been a slow process even though he was told it would take four or five years after beauty school to build a solid book. Instead of looking upon a complaint or observation from a client about his work as a learning experience, the insecure stylist dwells on the comment to the point of anxiety.

"But what if its five years from now and I don't have any more clients?"

"And what if Mrs. Kros tells all her friends that I'm a lousy hairdresser?"

"And what if I run into some of my former clients at the mall?"

Poor Richard! The young stylist could have chosen to use his thoughts to build himself up by visualizing a full client base in five years, or thinking about Mrs. Jones, Mrs. Harris, Mrs. Gold and all of the other clients who do love him and who tell their friends about him.

Richard could change his thinking to realize the fact that all stylists have former clients and that a stylist will lose three out of five every year. And, yes, Richard some clients die. But please don't take them personally either.

Richard doesn't need to change his salon or his profession. He just needs to change his thinking!

YOU can change your life most simply by changing your thoughts. Think about it! Your thoughts are real things. Henry Ford concluded that, "Believe you can or believe you can't; either way you'll be correct!" And the philosopher Baruch Spinoza observed that, "For as long as you think that something is impossible, for that exact moment of time, it will be. But the moment you see that dream as being reachable, that is the defining moment that you go on to conquer your challenge."

The size of the challenges in front of us doesn't change. But the size of our thinking that we can rise above them can change. Your thoughts can take you up or down the mountain. Thoughts are real things. Use your thought bricks to build, rather than to destroy.

NOTES

Here are a few examples of how our thoughts can work against us. In *The Feeling Good Handbook*, Dr. David Burns points out 10 forms of twisted thinking.

1. **All or nothing thinking.** Seeing things in black and white. When a client doesn't come back, thinking, "I can't hold on to any clients," rather than, "Unfortunately I, like most stylists, lose some clients. I'll do my best to see that it doesn't happen again."

2. **Overgeneralization.** Using "always" and "never" in your thinking.

3. **Mental filter.** Picking out a single negative detail in an event and dwelling on it constantly. You relive the one dissatisfied client and forget about all of the positive clients.

4. **Discounting the positive.** Rejecting positive experiences by thinking they "don't count."

5. **Jumping to conclusions.** Without checking it out, you think that someone doesn't like your work, or you.

6. **Magnification.** You exaggerate the importance of your problems or shortcomings.

7. **Emotional reasoning.** You assume that your negative thoughts and emotions are true reflections of the way things really are.

NOTES

8. **"Should" statements.** Thinking that things should be the way you think they should be.

9. **Labeling yourself.** Instead of thinking, "I made a mistake," labeling yourself like, "I'm a loser!"

10. **Personalization and blame.** Thinking yourself responsible for an event that isn't entirely under your control. "Our salon is struggling because of me."

You become what you think about. Put a stop sign up to your negative thoughts and reroute them in ways that they will build you and your salon.

* * * *

16

NOTES

Welcome Salon Changes As Refreshing Opportunities

"Progress always involves risk. You can't steal second base and keep your foot on first."

—Frederick Wilson

"Starting next week staff, we will be opening an extra day to accommodate the clients who have different needs."

Sam's words were received with a plethora of emotional reactions. Sam, the go-getter owner, saw great opportunities for his salon staff to grow by accommodating the changing nature of their clients' demand in their city. His recent salon survey clearly showed that his clientele had a preference for an early in the week service. The visionary devised a practical program to satisfy the clients in his area.

The open-minded leader offered stylists to choose who would work the Mondays. But he did need two stylists on the floor. Carla and Pat immediately volunteered to work the extra day as the rest of the staff breathed a sigh of relief. The two passionate salon professionals were always the first ones to see the refreshing opportunities change can bring.

"Sam, I have a thought. Could we open up early on Mondays, say seven o'clock for the client on her way to work at the start of the week?" Carla chimed.

Pat added, "How about a Monday-only discount on some of our chemical services?"

Sam was enthusiastic about the young stylists ideas, as the rest of the staff stared into space, dreaming of all of the problems change would create and secretly hoping the ideas would fail.

Carla and Pat were also staring into space, visualizing the opportunities of increasing their clientele and the service income they were going to produce for their salon, and themselves.

YOU probably have some family members or neighbors who get grouchy at all these changes taking place around them. They spend their lives bitter, complaining and sitting on the couch wishing that things would go back to the way they were when they were in their twenties in the "good old days." Not very fun to be around, are they? They are stuck in the past mud.

You've also seen "haircutters" who are in that same old rut who are going to work to make money to pay bills. And who hate and resist that new computer system, or that new coloring system. They don't realize it, but they begin looking like those relatives and neighbors who are stuck.

NOTES

You've seen salons where the drapes are dirty, the retail is dusty and the place has lost its luster. That's not very inspiring for either staff or clients.

And then you observe the passionate salon professionals, the builders. They are open to every new idea and they are excited by change. Change brings out their passion. They know how invigorating it is just to put up the showcase of the new professional products and wait for the perming class coming on Monday. The "haircutters" sit in the back, fold their arms resisting growing from new ideas, while the passionate salon professionals bring their notepads, and themselves, to life.

When you think of it every great moment of our life was a moment of change. Make it a point to make small changes every day to reinvigorate your whole mind and body. Take a walk at lunch, or drive home a different way or be determined to listen to some new music, or try new looks. Force yourself to get refreshment from change, not to be the couch potato fighting newness.

* * * *

PROCESS IV

"BE DRIVEN FROM WITHIN"

The "Haircutter"	The Passionate Salon Professional
17. "Nobody motivates me in my salon."	17. "Motivation comes from within."
18. "I have so many faults and weakness and can't do anything right."	18. "I focus on my strengths and talents. I find that putting my best foot forward keeps me going."
19. "Why do I have to go to classes?"	19. "Every class makes me better."
20. "Maybe I'll go to the staff meeting."	20. "I'll take notes at our meeting because there is always something I can use later."

17

Be Your Own Best Motivation Source Because You Are Always With You

*"Champions aren't made in gyms.
They are made from something they have
deep inside them — a desire,
a dream, a vision.
They have to have the skill, and the will.
But the will must be stronger than the skill."*

—Muhammad Ali

After twenty-two years in the salon industry, the highly professional Lorraine is well aware of her strengths as a stylist. She thanks the manager who informs her that her service income is five times the national average.

"Compliments are nice, but what really stokes me is when my heart becomes part of a style, knowing that I have done the best I possibly can. And, it may

NOTES

sound crazy to others, but I get a great deal of satisfaction when I get to the salon twenty minutes early, thinking about my approach to each of my clients," Lorraine tells us.

Theresa, the well-read manager, is intrigued by her top stylist. "Lorraine amazes us all. Whether I'm here or not, her performance is consistent. She styles from her heart, she retails because she gets satisfaction out of seeing her clients continue looking great, and Lorraine is a great teacher to our staff. She can go on and on without needing a push from anyone. She's got it inside her." These words, "she's got it inside her," are true reflections of a passionate salon professional."

Lorraine's has given herself the ultimate gift — motivation — a gift that keeps on giving — because it's always within.

YOU. What would you do if, from this moment on, for the rest of your life, no one ever again approved of your actions, applauded you, appreciated you, or even said to you, "Good job?"

Would you still survive? Would you go crazy for approval? Would you doubt yourself endlessly? Would you be less secure?

It has been said that at twenty we are devastated when others are talking about us. And at forty, we have worked it through and know that we can deal

with others talking about us. And, at sixty it hits us that others weren't even talking about us when we were twenty!

The haircutter needs to be pushed, punished, or praised by others. Psychologists call this "extrinsic motivation," because the person's source of motivational strength is outside of her. The passionate salon professional is driven from within. This person's "intrinsic motivation," assures everyone that she can be counted on. She does not need to be pushed to get the job done or be on time, because her motivational push comes from within.

Curiously, intrinsic motivation, or inner drive, is the single biggest predictor of a stylist's future growth because it does not depend on strong motivation, encouragement, or inspiration from others.

Be driven from within. Because you always have you!

*   *   *   *

18

Act Out of
Your Best Self

*"You are at least as great, as the greatest
achievement of your life"*

—Lewis Losoncy

Rosie, John's long-term client, beamed as she told him about her upcoming wedding plans. She was looking forward to having John style her hair the day of the wedding. As she explained her thoughts on an intricate up style to John that she would like on that her day, he realized that he would not be the one in the salon performing it. One of John's core strengths was his ability to know his own limitations, and he understood that sometimes you have to say "no" to build your business and stay credible.

John explained to Rosie that up styles were not his strong points the way working with a blow dryer and curling irons were. And then his face lit up as he enthusiastically referred his client to Margie, the well

NOTES

respected updo stylist in the booth rental salon. John's attitude was that the salon is there for client satisfaction, and he well remembers the clients that Margie referred to him in the past.

Amy, a stylist in the same salon was more concerned about her own income than the welfare of the client. She abhorred perms. Amy's wraps were atrocious as well as her body language when performing them. Her monetary greed took over recommending clients to other stylists. She was a short-term thinker who allowed the negatives to guide her actions. John was a passionate salon professional who knew not only his strengths, but the salon's strengths, and his desire to see a satisfied client far exceeded his need to be the one to provide the service.

YOU can focus on your strengths, or you can dwell on your weaknesses. Which choice will work better for you? Give your positive self at least equal time in your mind that you give your negative self. Do a little self-encouragement. Answer the following questions:

1. What are some things I accomplished that have given me personal satisfaction? Consider achievements as a student, as a friend, as a volunteer, as an athlete, a parent, or any other area of your life. List 3.

    a) _____

    b) _____

    c) _____

NOTES

2. What are your 3 most important assets?

   a) _____

   b) _____

   c) _____

3. What was the greatest achievement of your life? What qualities did it take for you to achieve that great accomplishment?

4. What is the biggest thing that you worked hard at to achieve and finally did? What was inside you to do that?

5. When did you fail at something, and instead of giving up, you pushed yourself forward, by yourself? What strengths did you need to keep going?

   Review your list. This is who you are. Keep these answers with you, at all times, and when you are discouraged, review your list of strengths and you will gain strength from within.

   Always put your best foot forward, and it will keep your passion going!

                  *   *   *   *

19

Education
Is Your Fastest Way
To A Better Future

*"The best cosmetic in the world is an active
mind that is always finding something new."*

—Mary Meek Atkeson

NOTES

Vilma was convinced that many people leave their stylist because of the boredom of getting the same old thing — even when the client asks for something different. Vilma would passionately talk to her salon team about the importance of education.

The caring salon manager beams, "Educational techniques are the equivalent of carpenter's tools in a tool box. The right tool makes the job easier whether you're building a house or hanging a picture. In the same way, a variety of techniques will stimulate the stylist in many ways of either designing a completely new style, or transforming a client's current one."

NOTES

Sheri of Topeka, Kansas writes, "I was locked in a rut where it seemed that all of my clients started to look the same. I hadn't been to a hair show in years because I felt that they were just being entertaining. But, after listening to the happiest stylist in our salon, I decided to go with her to a show with a different attitude. Changing my thinking worked. Even styles I didn't like at the show, taught me something. I now read Trade magazines, consumer magazines, watch styling videos and I feel that my haircutting basics have grown way beyond what they were a few years ago. And so has my income!"

Education is your fastest way to a better future! Education is a key tool for passionate salon professionals.

YOU might consider a new class in hairstyling to be similar to buying a new dress. As a dress gives you a different shape, texture, feel and look to your personal style, a styling class does the same for your professional style. And sometimes the old styles just need to be put behind us.

In any industry, education is always positive and encourages growth. It has been said that education is the fastest way to get to the front of the line. Education keeps you aware of new changes and new opportunities. Education prevents you from getting stagnant and stuck. Education breathes new life into you. If you want to find out the latest advances or styles, just take a class and it will open up new doors.

In order to have your clients feel as though you are on your toes and you are giving them the best service and styles available, they have to feel that you know exactly what you are doing. Education now, and in the future, gives you the confidence to maintain the edge in a fast paced industry.

* * * *

NOTES

20

Always Sit Up Front In Life!

NOTES

*"If a man constantly aspires,
is he not elevated?*

—Thoreau

The downtown Philadelphia stylist Cary always was one for sitting at the head of the class, never to be a show off, but rather, to take everything in, and to not miss a word of the lecture or seminar. The note taker always respected the person at the head of the class because he was impressed with anyone who had knowledge of their industry.

Cary once took a class on Shakespeare. The professor was excellent and Cary was in awe. Professor Celucci recited a soliloquy from Romeo and Juliet word for word, not even needing the book. Cary sat, right there at the head of the class and took in every word, every syllable.

"When you sit right up front, you don't miss a thing. It gives you the opportunity to actively participate in engaging questions and answers with the professor," the studious intellectual concluded. About ten years past and Cary ran into a fellow student who he did not remember. The fellow student was talking to her grandmother when she heard a voice from across the room. She approached Cary and asked, "Did you ever take a class on Shakespeare at Temple University?"

"Yes, I did."

"She continued, "I could never forget your voice. You always sat in front and asked the most interesting questions. I admired your passion for learning."

When you literally or figuratively sit up front in life, your passion comes through and others do notice. The beauty industry is no exception. When you do this with your clients they will feel your passion and be right up front there with you.

YOU know Joy. You may be like her, in fact. Joy is a self-starter.

While working with a salon staff, at the end of the meeting the manager turned to her staff of nine stylists and told them of a professional distributor program that will be held in four weeks. The manager thought that it would be great if one or two team members could attend the meeting, and bring the information back to the salon. Everyone looked down, except for the youngest stylist there. Her name was Joy.

"Well Mrs. T, I know that I am the youngest one here and everyone else should have the right to go first. But if others are busy, I'd really like to go to the show." Everyone agreed that the 20 year-old would represent the salon.

A number of years later, I (Dr. Lew) was giving a salon psychology speech in Baltimore, and the first one to arrive was a young stylist who was working hard pulling the cellophane off her cassettes to record the session. She was sitting right up in the front row. A few seconds later, she walked over to the podium, shook my hand and introduced herself with, "Dr. Lew I know you don't remember me but a few years ago you were in our salon and we met. My name is...."

"No need to go on," I enthusiastically responded. "Your name is Joy. We will never forget your love of education."

Joy's previous salon had closed down, and she was managing a salon in the Washington DC area.

Joy sat up front wherever she went. The others, in the back, are tenuous, not sure if they are going to commit to grow, or skip out at the first break. The front row seater arrives early and gets everything he or she can out of every experience in life.

We have seen front row seaters in every city from Portland, Maine to Portland, Oregon, from Jacksonville, Florida to Moberly, Missouri to El Paso, Texas and Camloops, British Columbia, Zagreb, Croatia to Perth, Australia. Front row seaters are linked by their passion. Join in!

NOTES

Sit up front at the seminar, in the church, and be the first one to volunteer to make your family, team or salon a better place. When you sit up front, you hear the life changing news first. Front row seaters are the first signs of passionate salon professionals.

* * * *

PART

CLIENT PASSION

PROCESS V: "BE AVAILABLE"

PROCESS VI: "TAKE EACH PERSON ONE STEP HIGHER"

PROCESS V

"BE AVAILABLE"

The "Haircutter"	The Passionate Salon Professional
21–30 "I do hair."	21. "I walk over to my client and welcome her. I want her to know I am happy to see her."
	22. "I try to be safe and non-critical of her words, her ideas, or even her hair."
	23. "I listen for the feelings under my client's words."
	24. "I immediately try to find things that I have in common with my client."
	25. "I never disagree with my client. I stay as tactful as possible without showing we disagree."
	26. "If my client is expressive and speaks fast, I do the same. If she is shy, I back off a bit. Everyone has their own comfort zone."
	27. "I reassure my clients that I will be here if she has a problem."
	28. "I think that it is important to do what you said you would do."
	29. "Its motivating to notice something special and unique about each client."
	30. "The client doesn't know about how great she'll look with your new service. So I emphasize its value by becoming enthusiastic about it."

21

Your Welcoming Skills Open People Up

"A kind word is like a spring day."

—Russian Proverb

You know Laura because she reminds you of the morning sunshine.

"You see its just how you say, 'Good morning,' to someone or how you smile and make eye contact that definitely opens up the people door. When I arrive at the salon in the morning, I say, 'Hi,' to at least ten people at the Seattle Coffee Bar. Make that another five or six in the office building elevator. Most people just stare at the numbers as each floor goes by with that good old statue-like gaze — as though the numbers were people."

"In the salon Laura greets every single client in such a way that each person thinks that Laura has been waiting for just them. Frankly some of the jealous stylists think she is a phony, but even they want

NOTES

to be with her! When meeting a client, she is sensitive to whether the client wants to shake hands, or stay at a distance. She seems to have ESP."

To that, we add that Laura is a PSP who has ESP!

YOU have experienced a first visit to a salon where the receptionists tells you something like "go back to Sandy now." You walked back into the styling area, looking around until someone shouts, "sit down."

And, by contrast, you've been in salons where the passionate salon professional comes out to greet you with a big, wide smile, looks you in the eyes and welcomes you to the salon. Perhaps on the way back she introduced you to a few other team members complimenting certain skills that each has and soon you are a member of a new caring family of people who love working together.

The difference between the two salons is huge. The first impression that you receive is long lasting, whether it is positive or negative. The difference was that the first salon was filled with "haircutters." The second salon was housed with passionate salon professionals who open people up with welcoming skills.

Here are a few suggestions to increase your welcoming skills:

1) Develop your ability to make and hold eye contact with your clients.

2) Smile while looking into the other person's eyes.

3) Introduce yourself while shaking the client's hand or touching her lightly on the shoulder. Sense what she feels comfortable with and adjust yourself accordingly.

4) Use your name while shaking her hand making sure she hears your name and she gets it.

5) If she has a difficult name which you are not sure how to pronounce show her the respect by asking her until you have it. The more difficult her name, the less she hears it because most people are afraid to try. Show her you care enough to get it because you know that it is important to her.

6) Guide her safely to your styling station.

* * * *

PSP

NOTES

22

Your Warmth Skills Invite Clients To Feel Safe

"The greatest motivational act one person can do for another is to listen"

—Roy E. Moody

The young Goth client walked dimly into the suburban salon's waiting room. Her matching black eye makeup and skirt along with her knee high boots, on this mid-summer's day, caused some clients to sneer in judgment while others tensed up. The big hearted stylist Tiffany walked over to Melissa with her usual friendly smile and extended hand. "Hi Melissa, I'm Tiffany, welcome to Cynergy. Let's go back to my station and discuss your Thermal Straightening before you are shampooed." Melissa gives a broad smile while offering a soft, sweet "Thank you" and follows Tiffany.

NOTES

Tiffany's warmth not only relaxes Melissa, but eases the tension in the whole waiting room.

YOU can walk into a salon and within seconds feel whether the stylist you are with is a warm or a cold person. What is the difference?

The warm passionate salon professional smiles, is easy to be with, is safe and you sense she is listening to you rather than judging you. The warm stylist has an open body language and a soothing tone of voice. You could say that the warm stylist is "with you." The warmer the salon professional, the more honest the dissatisfied customer will be in expressing her concerns. Consequently, warm stylists can correct problems and save the customer for the salon.

A warm salon professional is a welcomed sight in this sometimes stressed, frazzled world. Being with a person who centers on your interests is rare and rewarding. Here are a few suggestions to increase your warmth:

1) Think of the warmest person you know. Think of the coldest person you know. Identify the differences between the two. Imagine yourself developing the sensitivity and the style of the warmer person.

2) Become a passion skills scientist. Wherever you go, rate people in your own mind to their levels of warmth on a scale from 1 to 5. A score of 1 indicates a cold, detached individual who is critical, cynical and judgmental. A 5 represents a warm person with whom you feel safe.

3) When you are with a client, center on her interests without bringing in your story.

4) Communicate warm involvement through your facial expressions to show that you are in tune with the moment-to-moment ideas and feelings of the other person (laughing with your client or expressing concern when she is anxious or worried).

5) Have an open body language (lean forward, soft touch, open arms, smiling face).

6) Block out all other distractions when the other speaks.

A passionate salon profession is a warm person who often hears something like, "I've never told anybody this before, but I...."

* * * *

23

Your Empathy Skills Help People Feel Understood

"Tolerance and patience should not be read as signs of weakness. They are signs of strength."

Valda was both frustrated and nervous about her forthcoming African safari. One of the few people she shared her fears with was her stylist Joe, who she saw every week. She initially centers her conversation on what she would do with her hair in the jungle climate. Her empathic stylist senses deeper concerns about her trip than her hair.

Valda: *Its going to take 24 hours to get to Tanzania. Will I still look good when I get off the plane. You know the only thing I can do in those who knows what, scary conditions is wash my hair.*

Joe: *Valda, a texture service to give your hair body that is soft enough to last a couple of months is all you would need.*

Valda: I guess I shouldn't even be thinking about my hair with everything else going on like terrorism, air safety, disease. I just want to get home safe.

Joe: You sound anxious (empathy) about the trip, Valda.

Valda: (eyes moisten) To tell you the truth Joe I dread going, but I'm doing it for my husband who has a life long dream of going on a safari. He even offered to go by himself if I was afraid, but I never would forgive myself if something happened to him.

Joe: Your love transcends your fears (empathy). Deep down, I'll bet you feel thrilled (empathy) that you could do this for Jim. Your selflessness is admirable, Valda.

Valda: Thanks for listening Joe. I feel so stupid talking to anyone else about it. I'd love that texture.

Joe: I promise not to tell anyone. Let's get to work.

YOU are experiencing empathy when you are hearing your client's feelings under her words. When the haircutter and the passionate salon professional with empathy listen to a client say, "I want something new," the haircutter starts thinking what that new look could be. The passionate salon professionals experiences the feelings under her words, perhaps boredom from the past looks or excitement about a new look. By using empathy skills and communicating back to your client that you heard her feelings under her words, her head starts nodding and smiling because she feels understood at a deeper level. Then you can proceed more safely with her to consult about the new look.

NOTES

Empathic skills are the skills of not only sensing your client's feelings but communicating her feelings back to her. Sensitive listening helps you to understand the other person's perspective and empathic responding helps you communicate your client's feelings to her.

Here are a few suggestions to further develop your skills of empathic responding:

1) Demonstrate an understanding of the facts about your client's world.

2) Ask yourself, "If I was experiencing these same facts she told me she is experiencing, what would I possibly be feeling?"

3) Communicate those feelings back to her until she shows you that you understand her feelings,

    e.g. "That must have been *frustrating* (feeling word) for you"

    e.g. "That *hurts*, doesn't it?"

    e.g. "I'll bet you're *excited*."

* * * *

24

Your Mutuality Skillls Create Bonds Between Yourself And Your Client

*"The more I think you are like me,
the more I like you."*

Sandi is unbelievable! Put her in a room full of strangers and she is going to establish a common bond with them within a few minutes of meeting! Her special skill of making immediate connections with anyone has accelerated her growth as a hairstylist. What's her secret?

Tune in to a recent dialogue Sandi has with her first time client Karrie.

Sandi: *I noticed you are reading a book on personal finance. Have you ever read any Suze Oreman's books?*

Karrie: *I sure have, she is a great writer. I like the simplicity of her concepts.*

NOTES

Sandi: *Me too! Personal finance was a jigsaw puzzle to me before reading her books.*

Karrie: *She's doing a seminar at the Academy in two weeks, want to go?*

Mutuality skills are simple and powerful techniques to detect common interests with clients that can lead to long term friendships in and out of the styling chair!

YOU have clients who are well connected in your community, don't you? You mention someone's name, and she knows him. She is going to the mayor's house for a party, then to volunteer at the children's center and spent some time with the state representative. How do some people get around so easily? You can bet they have mutuality skills.

Mutuality skills are the skills of finding common bonds, links or similarities with others. Mutuality skills are based upon the similarity-liking principle, which suggests that the more I feel you are like me, the more I like you.

What often appears like small talk can play a big role in building connections and long-term relationships with clients. Finding out that you and your client have a soccer-playing daughter or a son who is applying to college brings you together more quickly.

Here are a few ways to develop your mutuality skills:

NOTES

1) When meeting someone immediately look for common interests, common experiences, common backgrounds, common hobbies, movies, sports, books, etc. Each connection is another relationship seed.

2) Share those commonalities back with your client.

3) Keep a small index card about each client and write on the card, "Commonalities," make a note on your mutual interests, etc. review the card before meeting your client the next time and open up your session with, "How's your soccer star?"

4) Start using the words, "We," or "People like us enjoy..."

* * * *

25

Your Agreement Skills Get You On The Same Side

"We cannot change anything until we accept it. Condemnation does not liberate, it oppresses."

—Carl Jung

Sherry's back for her salon service after attending an animal rights protest and is on a rampage about the annual deer shoot to control their population. Her stylist, Hope is troubled because she feels there is a need for deer population control. As Sherry rants on, Hope finds that she can't take it any longer and explodes at her client — because a deer ran in front of her best friend's car, laying her up for weeks. An argument ensues until Lucia calmly intervenes and starts talking to Sherry while encouraging Hope to relax in the break room.

Sherry: *All I said was that is unfair the deer have nowhere to go because of the developer's greed building houses all over the deer's land.*

Lucia: *Sherry, I agree. Animals have rights too. I have two dogs and a cat. Do you have any pets? (Agreement skill)*

Sherry: *Yes, I have two dogs as well.*

Lucia: *How old are they?*

Sherry: *I have two pugs, three and seven.*

Lucia: *My cat is seven also. It's sure easy to get attached in seven years with your pet.*

Sherry: *(Relaxes) I know.*

Lucia: *Did you know that Hope has a pug?*

Sherry: *Really! I like the way she does my hair. Please have her come back. Sometimes I get too passionate about my beliefs. I'm sorry.*

Lucia: *I'll get her for you. Ask her about Winston, her pug.*

YOU have experienced someone stopping your enthusiastic idea with words, "Let me play devil's advocate," haven't you? The very phrase creates a confrontation. Those words are never included in any human relation's book because they turn people off.

The agreement skill does just the opposite. This positive skill turns people on to speak more and to feel more in sync with you. The agreement skill involves listening to your client with the conscious determination to keep you and her in the agreement mode. Ultimate rapport is experienced when the stylist and client are in the agreement rhythm. When the stylist and client are in harmony with their ideas, feelings, thoughts and plans, they are in the agreement mode.

NOTES

The passionate salon professional is sensitive to offer new information in such a way that highlights their points of agreement. The stylist makes sure that the mood is one that feels like, "We agree on mostly everything."

How do you use the agreement skill?

1) When your client says something with which you disagree the natural tendency is to answer by starting with the word "But." "But," like "Let me play devil's advocate," puts you two into a disagreement mode. Chances are she won't even hear what you are about to say because she is rebuilding her argument anticipating what you are about to say next.. So how do you replace "But," for the purpose of staying in the agreement mode? Simple. Use the agreement word, "And" instead of "But."

2) Look for areas of agreement, even in points of disagreement.

3) Sense common interests and experiences.

4) Identify common strengths

NOTES

5) Emphasize common ways of thinking

6) Be sensitive to moments in which you begin experiencing each other as being on opposite sides, and quickly re-route to avoid entering the disagreement mode.

7) To keep your client from feeling the subconscious uncomfortable feeling associated with saying, "No," structure your questions in such a way as to get the more positive, "Yes," answers

8) And never play devil's advocate again!

* * * *

26

Your Mirroring Skills Create Synchronicity

"Show me a man who cannot be bothered to do little things, and I'll show you a man who can't be trusted to do big things."

—Lawrence Bell

You know someone like Lisa. When you are with her you feel she is so in tune with you. Nothing else in the world matters to her but you. And you can especially see it in her body language and vocabulary. Lisa is listening in a relaxed face-to-face consultation with Mrs. Silver, her soft-spoken client. Lisa's voice softens. Mrs. Silver lifts her hands up by her ears describing a horrible color she once had, and Lisa mirrors, duplicating Mrs. Silver's hand placement on the side of her own head. Lisa is communicating through her mirroring skills that she understands her client and is in sync with her client through her own body language and voice tone.

NOTES

Lisa's next client is the outspoken Jane whose animated style, fast and loud ramblings bellow throughout the salon. Everyone knows when Jane is present. Lisa adjusts to Jane in order to (1) build rapport, and (2) calm her down. Lisa speaks fast, like Jane, and louder than she did with Mrs. Silver. Then Lisa tactfully starts speaking softer and slower to bring Jane's decibel levels down.

Lisa knows that mastering mirroring skills allows you to relate to anyone, introvert or extrovert, by getting in touch with them in a style with which they feel most comfortable.

YOU can watch two people from a distance and guess whether they are connecting or not just by observing their body language. When two people are in rapport they subconsciously start to mirror and match each other's body language. You can use this information to consciously start developing the passion skill of mirroring. Mirroring is literally being a mirror to your client's words, speed of speech, facial and body expressions and tendency to get closer or more distant in the relationship. The passionate salon professional takes time to master this skill of mirroring to create synchronicity with her clients.

Here are a few suggestions of behaviors for you to work on to master the mirroring passion skill.

1) Listen to your client's speed of speech. The faster she speaks, the more quickly you speak with her. If she speaks slowly deliberately slow down your

speech. If you catch yourself finishing her sentences, let that be a signal to you to stop, pause, slow down and speak more at her pace.

2) Study your client's amount of body expressiveness, especially her arms and hands. The more expressive your client is, the more expressive you become. If she doesn't express herself at all, be more conservative with you arms and hands.

3)   Model your client's facial expressions. When she shows joy with a smile and lifts her hands up by her face, mirror her by doing exactly the same.

4) When she folds her hands, fold your hands.

5) Practice mirroring in your everyday work.

6) It is not unusual when you meet a first-time client, after mirroring her for a few minutes, to hear her ask, "Don't I know you from somewhere?"

Get passionate about mirroring.

* * * *

27

Your Positioning Skills Put You In A Safe Place In Your Client's Mind

"Show people you have nothing to hide, and they will open up to you as well."

Consider these two stylists to identify the one with positioning skills in meeting a new client.

Client: *How long have you worked here?*

First Stylist: *A while.*

Client: *Where did you go to beauty school?*

First Stylist: *Out West.*

Client: *Are you married?*

First Stylist: *Kind of…*

Now contrast the first stylist with the second stylist who has mastered positioning skills.

Client: *How long have you worked here?*

Second Stylist: *Three years on the 15th of next month. I love it here. What a great caring team we have. I hope you meet the whole staff.*

Client: *Where did you go to beauty school?*

Second Stylist: *I went to school in Sacramento California, The Beauty College of California. We received a great, but tough, education there.*

Client: *Are you married?*

Second Stylist: *Yes, seven years to my wife Donna who is from Macon, Georgia. We have twin four year olds Sean and Damon.*

The client feels much safer with the second stylist because he appears to have nothing to hide. He is safely positioned in his first time client's mind and she is more willing to try a new look with him than with the first stylist who has a "fly by night" aroma about him — because he hasn't sensed the opportunity to safely position himself in her mind.

YOU have met clients who were very vague when you asked them specific questions.

Stylist: *Originally, where are you from?*

Client: *Oh, up North!"*

Stylist: *New England?*

Client: *No.*

While its perfectly fine for the paying client to resist being positioned, it makes rapport impossible and leaves the relationship unsettled and temporary.

As a stylist, positioning is a crucial passion skill to developing your relationship with your clients.

"First, I'm going to apply color, next I'll rinse it out and shampoo before applying a color-safe conditioner. Then I'll cut a nice style for you and spray in a gel before I blow dry. Finally I'll recommend the best professional products for your hair."

Positioning is creating opportunities to plant yourself clearly and safely in a comfortable spot in your client's mind and heart. When you are positioned, you become solid and clear, rather than vague and elusive to your client.

Here are a few other tips to develop your positioning skills:

1) Don't hesitate to share a little about your life if the person asks. This of course does not include personal phone number or address.

2) Let people know a little about your own interests if they express interest in knowing.

3) People who don't recall our names never get close to us — or we to them.

NOTES

* * * *

28

Your Credibility Skills Make You Trustworthy

"A 'no' uttered from deepest conviction is better and greater than a 'yes' merely uttered to please, or what is worse, to avoid trouble."

—Ghandi

Here is an example of how a passionate salon professional purposefully builds credibility with a first time client. (Notice how she sets the stage with six specific things she is going to do for her client).

Stylist: After talking with you, to offer you what you would like, there are seven things I'm going to do with your hair, Mrs. Greenshingle. First, I'm going to apply our beautiful professional color, second wash it out and shampoo, third apply conditioner, fourth styling aids, fifth create a nice style, and sixth blow dry your hair and finally recommend the best professional products for your hair.

After each treatment, the stylist reminds her client, "Fourth, as I promised, I am going to...." Notice in

NOTES

one appointment this unknown stylist has revealed how she plans ahead and how she did exactly what she said she would do. Credibility builds clientele and gives you an edge over the average "haircutter."

YOU have credibility when your client believes you. Credibility is believability. Credibility involves effectively communicating two things, "I can be trusted to do what I said I would do," and "I know what I am talking about." You might say the formula for credibility then is:

Credibility = Trustworthiness + Knowledge.

The passionate salon professional is obsessed with working hard at small things to build big trust and earn credibility. Building trust is actually relatively easy for a stylist to do. Think about it for a moment. Who do you trust? You trust people who, in the past, did what they said they would do and had it done by the time they said it would be done.

There are many ways to help earn credibility with your clients:

1) Tell your client who tries a new service and is unsure if she likes it that you will call her at a certain time during the week to see how she is feeling then. Then go out of your way to call at exactly that time. Listen to her surprised and thankful voice and reaction to your promise delivered. Credibility forever!

2) Communicate your knowledge and accuracy by being as detailed as possible with your client. If

you show your attention to details, and your customer notices your concern about the details, she doesn't have to be worried herself.

NOTES

3) When you go to an educational program, always, always talk about what you learned to each of your clients for a few seconds. Let each client know that her stylist is a passionate professional who loves education.

4) Return things that you borrow by the time you said you would return them.

5) Remember:

Credibility (Believability) = Trustworthiness + Knowledge

* * * *

29

Your Personalizing Skills Turn Your "9 O'Clock Client" Into A Person

"The difference between ordinary and extraordinary is that little extra."

—Joe Santy

Pete is Larry's Thursday 4:30 appointment every four weeks. It'll be "just a trim." Pete is an executive with a local auto parts manufacturer. Larry, his stylist went to a local church to hear a speaker that attracted 2,200 attendees. As the choir of 120 took the stage, to Larry's surprise, Pete was one of the members. Two weeks later, when Pete came in for his cut, Larry sung the praises of Pete's choir to the rest of the staff comparing his harmonic voice to some of the greats. He noticed Pete's big wide smile.

Until then Larry viewed Pete as his 4:30 Thursday. Through this experience, Pete became a person to

NOTES

Larry, and Larry became a person to Pete, deepening both of their relationships. Larry noticed that Pete referred another choir member to Larry.

YOU have a social security number, a checking account number, a phone number, an insurance account number, and a case number when you have an accident. You are a number wherever you go. And then you come into the salon and hear, "Are you my 9 o'clock?" In today's world of small business, especially one in which human contact and touch are involved, it is important that everyone strive to find ways to get away from a de-personalizing approach to people. Sensitive salons, for example are teaching their staffs the personalizing skills to help each client feel special, unique, respected and important.

My (Dr. Lew) high school guidance counselor, Fr. Pete was the greatest personalizer I ever met in my life. When he saw you in the hallway he'd smile, lift his hand up and say, "There he is!" Everyone thought that Fr. Pete was waiting to see them. He successfully communicated to each student, "You're the appointment I was waiting to see all day." And he truly meant it.

As people walk into your salon off the cold streets and you take the time to give them that Fr. Pete personalized greeting, you make their day. "There she is," or "Here comes my special friend," or "Here comes hoops!" to the high school athlete or "How's the greatest grandmother in the world?" to the proud grandma, you help the person feel respected, important, special and unique in their eyes. With your personalizing skills, you are not going to lose this client.

Here are a few other tips to increase your personalizing skills:

1) Observe a positive uniqueness in each client.

2) Remember small positive details about the person's life. Write these details down on your index card on the client's personality.

3) Prepare each session with a short, tailored greeting to your client.

4) Whenever possible, create positive nick names for your clients that show you think about them.

* * * *

NOTES

30

NOTES

Your Enthusiasm Skills Add Energy To Your Relationship And Your Services

"You can do anything if you have enthusiasm. Enthusiasm is the yeast that makes your hopes rise to the stars."

—Henry Ford

To Sherron, shampoo is just soap in the bottle. No big deal, and neither are her retail sales.

To Susan, shampoo gives the hair life, bounce, manageability, control, eliminates dandruff, and solves problems. And the list of benefits that Susan can enthusiastically explain is as endless as her client list.

Susan is a passionate salon professional! And her product sales reflect that.

YOU can watch two stylists describe the exact same professional product to a client. One gives the name of the product, while the other brings the product to life with her enthusiasm. The passionate salon professional adds value to the product by engaging the client's emotions, hopes and dreams with the product. The tenth passion skill is enthusiasm. How do you become enthusiastic? Simple: You become enthusiastic!

1) Wake up enthusiastically in the morning because you got another day of opportunity to cosmetically and psychologically transform self-images and destinies of fellow human being.

2) Answer your phone enthusiastically telling people you are happy to hear from them and they are important to you.

3) Listen enthusiastically by getting excited or concerned about what is important to others.

4) Smile enthusiastically showing people you are full of life and happy to be with them.

5) Walk enthusiastically to demonstrate that you are going places, you have a direction and a purpose

6) Speak enthusiastically showing people that you have something important to say and giving people the energy and desire to listen to you

7) Use enthusiastic words and sentences. Instead of saying you are "OK," let people know you are doing, "Great!" You can tell someone he is doing a "Good job," or you can enthusiastically thank him for his, "Fantastic performance."

8) Get into an enthusiastic mindset when facing a challenge with a client. Always be there with the reassuring phrase, "No problem, we can handle this."

* * * *

 # PROCESS VI

"TAKE EACH PERSON ONE STEP HIGHER"

The "Haircutter"	The Passionate Salon Professional
31. "I give clients looks that I like."	31. "I give clients what they need."
32. "I point out my client's problems."	32. "I focus on my client's strengths."
33. "I cut hair."	33. "Its important to notice the small changes clients make in their lives."
34. "If someone says, 'Just a trim,' I won't push them."	34. "I tell my clients, 'I have been thinking about a new look for you.' They are complimented."
35. "If my client is hesitant about changing her hair, I let it go."	35. "If my client seems unsure about a new look, I listen and help them through the decision. If I sense they really want it, I'm their encourager!"

31

Be A Client-Centered (Rather Than A Self-Centered) Passionate Salon Professional

"Its is only as we develop others that we permanently succeed."

—Harvey S. Firestone

"What do you want? Same thing as last time?" is one approach, but consider the passionate salon professional Edie's client-centered way.

Unlike the haircutter, Edie couples the skills of empathy and personalizing in her consultations to give her clients the ultimate client-centered recommendations. She goes beyond the hair, realizing that a client's hair is one part of the whole client. Edie hopes her recommendations will be acceptable to the client.

NOTES

Before asking the three important questions regarding hair, Edie likes to get a feel for the whole picture. Edie learns about her client's unique personality, lifestyle, styling abilities, change comfort level, previous negative and positive salon experiences and desired looks. Then Edie proceeds with the three questions:

(1) What do you like most about your hair? This immediately helps Edie to build on the positives the client feels about her hair, increasing rapport.

(2) What do you like least about your hair? This is the selling/solution question that Edie makes her recommendations with.

(3) What do you expect this service to do? This let's Edie know if her client's expectation level aligns with what she is physically capable of doing with their hair.

YOU know that if you are depressed and go to a dietitian, a minister, an aerobics expert and a psychologist, for help, you will probably hear four different recommendations to overcome your depression. That is because each professional makes a recommendation based upon his or her area of expertise (self-centered), rather than on what you need (client-centered). This is natural and experts in any profession have a natural bias for recommending specific treatments that they are most aware.

Self-centered recommendations are quite frequent in the cosmetology profession, as well. Stylists tend to recommend what they have been complimented on in the past. Consequently, many clients' appearances are not maximized because the self-centered recommendations are limited to what the stylists believe they do well. Stylists are not to be blamed for this. The way of overcoming self-centered recommendations is to learn as many different styles and approaches to perming and coloring techniques in order to be more well rounded. Also, the passionate salon professional's knowledge of the specific uniqueness, personality, lifestyle, change comfort level of the client, the more equipped she is to give a client-centered recommendation.

NOTES

Contrast the differences between the haircutter and the passionate salon professional.

Self-centered Recommending "Haircutter"	Client-centered Recommending Passionate Salon Professional
Recommends what I do well	Recommends what the client needs
Does robot like cutting	Believes in creativity, exploring alternatives, encourages new possibilities
Cuts in mass production	Individualizes cut, perm, color or style
Sees all clients the same way	Sees each client in unique, special ways
Focuses on hair	Focuses on each client's total self
Gives identical twins the same look	Treats each twin separately, giving the bank teller twin a dramatically different look than the artist twin

NOTES

No greater compliment can be paid to a client than to be touched by a passionate salon professional who has taken some time to listen, and to understand the client's (1) hair, (2) facial features, (3) physical features, (4) lifestyle, (5) profession, (6) change comfort level, (7) previous experiences with other looks, and to synergize that unique information into a customized client-centered recommendation.

* * * *

32

Sense And Share Your Client's Hair, Skin And Nail Strengths With Her

"Realize that now, in this moment of time,
you are creating.
You are creating your next moment.
That is what's real."

—Sara Paddison

Kathy was a 31 year-old blonde client who described the pain she experienced in salons for years by the stylists dwelling on her bad hair. Kathy explained, "Ever since I was a young child, I would go to the salon and get verbally abused by the hairdresser. I would be told, 'You have baby fine limp hair that could never be permed, never allow it to grow long and look horrible.' How do you think I felt? I mean, this stuff is growing out of my head. So to avoid the salon embarrassment, I started cutting my own hair."

Then a smile broke out on her face. "When I was 27, I decided to give the salon one more chance when

NOTES

I heard there was a positive and sensitive stylist in Northern New Jersey named Tommy. After arriving at the salon I was escorted to my chair and my tension was building. He walked over to my chair with a smile on his face, I spoke first and apologetically wished him good luck with this mess on my head. He stopped me in the middle of the apology and said, 'Kathy you have such a gorgeous face and beautiful cheek bones.' While running his fingers through my hair, he commented, 'Your hair is like silk. Cutting your hair will be a breeze.' Tommy discussed all of my special features that even I was unaware of. A few appointments later, Tommy even encouraged me to let him highlight my hair. He showed me how to take care of my hair, to respect it, to be proud of it. I feel like a winner when I am with Tommy. Now I travel four hours every few weeks to be with Tommy, the one person who gave my hair hope."

YOU have had teachers who marked the number wrong, rather than the number right. Chances are your dentist talked about your cavities, and your doctor centered in on the problems your test results uncovered. This deficiency, weakness or sickness focusing is giving way in many professions to a new model, a wellness, prevention and a human potential model. Centering on strengths instead of immediately spotting weaknesses not only creates a more positive experience for the patient or client, but helps the client feel more respected by the professional serving them. You have experienced stylists who center on what's wrong with their clients hair, often ignoring what's right; and what is possible in the talented hands with the talented tools of the passionate salon professional.

Passionate salon professionals are part of the more positive approach of focusing in on their client's hair, skin, nails, and life potential. The negatives are not ignored but are discussed with hope, optimism and a desire to bring out these possibilities.

NOTES

How do you use a strength focusing style in relating to your clients to give them more positive experiences with your salon and yourself?

1) Always start off with a compliment, noticing something that will lift the client's spirits.

2) When listening to your client's past negative experiences with her hair or a salon, show her that you understand her upset feelings. (You want to subtly communicate that you are sensitive and sure that this experience will not happen to her).

3) When she describes her hair, skin or nail problems, empathize, communicating back to her feelings while, at the same time, communicate your confidence that this issue has a resolution.

4) Talk up the strengths of her hair and the potential you see in her hair.

5) Make the strengths the theme and the problem just a small afterthought.

6) Always leave with a compliment and have a team member or two come in to support your positive approach.

NOTES

Interestingly, every recommendation and treatment you give will probably be the same regardless of whether you use the positive or negative approach. Changes in your emphasis on the positive and on your client's strengths will be what she remembers most in her heart about her experiences with you — her passionate salon professional.

* * * *

33

Spot Your Client's Small Changes, Efforts And Progress

"Judge not each day by the harvest you reap, but by the seeds you sowed."

—Robert Louis Stevenson

"How did your husband like your last cut, Charlotte?" Sandra eagerly asked.

"Sandy, my husband doesn't notice or if he does, he's never said, 'I like your hair.' Its frustrating that he doesn't notice, and after a week I can't take it any more and so I finally ask him. He doesn't notice a thing."

Sandra's brow furrowed; her eyes looked down as she bit her bottom lip. "I'm sorry," she whispered.

"Don't be! One of the great things I like about coming to you and Faces Salon is that you all notice and compliment the clients and each other's work.

NOTES

When my friend Sylvia had lost her first ten pounds the whole staff raved when she was in. She's lost another thirty pounds and only has five pounds to go. She had said that she was ready to give up before all the accolades she received here! Sandra, I appreciate when you notice and comment to me that I changed my make up, even when it's a subtle change. That conveys to me how much you care and notice about your clients. These little things really contribute to making Faces a great, warm, friendly, family-feeling salon for me!"

YOU too have seen behavioral and attitude changes in your client through your professional skills, and as well as through your encouragement, haven't you? When they look better, they feel better. Plus it goes further than that. When they look and feel better, their attitude and actions change in life. And because of your close and frequent contacts with her, you are often the first one to notice these changes.

"Wow, Brenda, you are looking great today."

"After the total makeover you gave me, I said to myself, all I have to do is lose a few pounds. I'm down five pounds since my last appointment."

These encouraging interactions are common when the passionate salon professional notices the small changes, efforts and improvements in her client. Its like her client is thinking "I'll make the extra effort because somebody cares about me."

NOTES

A stylist's influence is clearly not just on her adult clients. Children are especially inclined to respond to a stylist noticing her differences.

"I see you have your guitar."

"Yeah, remember when you cut my hair last time we talked about me playing a guitar, and you said you'd like to see it. I couldn't wait to show you."

Noticing a client's efforts, improvements and progress not only makes good human caring sense, but makes good business sense as well. In fact salon leaders of the future who transform their staffs into passionate salon professionals will be focusing much effort in educating and inspiring their staffs to lock up client loyalty by having their teams develop techniques to encourage their clients. And a big part of being an encouraging and passionate salon professional is to sensitively notice your client's efforts, improvements and progress.

Think about it. Don't you want your child to have not only a teacher with great knowledge in the subject matter, but also with great passion about the subject and the skills to encourage your child by noticing your child's efforts, improvements and progress?

How about your doctor? Wouldn't you prefer a doctor who notices improvements in cholesterol levels, blood pressure, etc? How about your priest, minister or rabbi? Of course.

When you notice small changes in your client, you are not only her stylist. You are her encourager!

NOTES

Chicago area passionate salon professional Colleen McEvoy notices everything about her clients. Colleen gets more referrals from her clients than any passionate salon professional we know.

* * * *

34

Dream Of New Looks For Your Client. What A Compliment To Her!

"When you make your client's dreams part of your dreams, both your destinies are changed."

—Joe Santy

It's one thing to say you're thinking about your clients. However, proving you've been dreaming about new looks for them feels great, and shows you value them, locking their loyalty in, sometimes for life!

Consider Alexa from Innovations in Honolulu. After servicing a client for a few times, if she feels they need a change, she proactively begins the process.

Reading the latest in consumer and trade magazines, a requisite for all passionate salon professionals,

NOTES

because it keeps them ahead with what's going on. She'll clip an image here, a color there, maybe a curl pattern or two to give her client an idea of the direction she'd like her to head in. The style doesn't have to be exact (nice if it was). However, it's just a guide to make the communication better between she and her client, and hard core proof that she truly was "dreaming of her client's new look."

YOU, as a passionate salon professional, have a very valuable tool. Your attention. Your attention is an added benefit that your client gets. And when you subtly show your client that you were thinking about her outside of the appointment, you reveal your caring and your passionate professionalism.

"I have been thinking about you."

"You have. What have you been thinking about?"

"I've been thinking about the perfect new look for you."

"Tell me about it!"

Along with noticing your client's efforts, improvements and progress, the encouraging and passionate salon professional already has a plan, before the appointment, for each client.

Arrive in the salon one-half hour early and get your passion up for the day's opportunities. Or, if you have time in the evening, prepare your client's new look plan the night before. Look over your client list.

NOTES

9:00 Mrs. Janis. Usually comes in for just a trim. Let me dream of a few versatile styles considering all of my services, from perming to coloring, highlighting, tone on tone color to manicuring to massage to skin care and aesthetics to my styling products, etc. Let me consider some change she is going through, eg. Starting college, going through a divorce, new job and tie the change in with the event. I'll tie in any positive changes she is making in her life, like joining the athletic club, taking long walks, or beginning a new diet.

This dialogue recently happened in a Reading, Pennsylvania salon:

"Hi, Mrs. Janis, I was thinking about you last night."

"You were?"

"I thought that since you were going back to school to finish your Bachelor's Degree in education, what new look can I design especially for you? I'll show you what I came up with and you can think about the new look for the next appointment."

"Hmm, why do we have to wait for our next appointment?"

The client thanked her passionate salon professional for not only the new look, but for thinking about her. What a compliment!

* * * *

35

You Are The Best Person To Encourage Your Client To "Go For It!"

"When you encourage another person, you change the world!"

—Lew Losoncy

Deirdre's passion for encouraging clients to "go for the new look," was as practical, as it was passionate.

"I build such a strong, convincing case for my client to take action and get that new look. Let me tell you just a few things I tell her."

"Whatever she asks for, I repeat back until I see her head nodding, indicating we both agree on that new look. Then I help her to imagine that new look in her mind, and make it easy for her to see that the change is not so drastic and that we do many of these services and they work perfectly. I help her to see how her

NOTES

new look will serve her better than her previous style, and even will tie it in with a new dress that she talked about. I offer guarantees for the longevity of the service and ease of styling to further relax her. I may even talk about previous testimonials of clients who had similar looks. Finally, I get her enthused not only about her new look but her new self. Usually by now the client's ready."

Could you say, "no," to Deirdre?

YOU are so, so much more than your client's hair-cutter. You notice changes in her attitude and her actions, you think about customized new looks based upon your professional techniques, tools and products and tie the new look into her lifestyle changes. Now the completion of your encouragement involves helping your anxious client to take action and, "go for it!"

When people were asked what qualities they saw in the most encouraging persons or stylists in their lives were, several clear patterns emerged. Study each one closely and use this as a checklist to become an even more encouraging and passionate salon professional.

My encourager...

1) really listened to me

2) thought I was special

3) noticed what was right with me instead of focusing on what's wrong with me

4) was enthusiastic about me and my life

NOTES

5) encouraged me to try new looks

6) sometimes even said, "you've got to do it. Trust me!"

7) recognized immediately when I needed a lift and was there for me

8) reassured me that things would be OK

9) was interested in me as person as well as a client

10) was a great teacher to me, taught me how to keep my hair looking great

11) was a positive upbeat person

12) accepted me even if I was upset or criticized him

13) remembered our previous conversations

14) was a terrific example. I even quit smoking because of her

We hope you have expanded your view of the opportunities the salon offers you. These include being a client-centered salon professional who senses and shares your client's strengths with her, who spots her small changes and efforts to improve her life, and who dreams of new looks for her while encouraging her to "go for it."

* * * *

Part

TEAM PASSION

PROCESS VII: "FIND YOUR PASSIONATE PURPOSE TOGETHER"

PROCESS VIII: "VALUE YOUR COMMUNITY MORE THAN YOUR EGO"

PROCESS IX: "PLAY WITH REALITY"

PROCESS X: "FIND YOUR WAY TOGETHER"

 **PROCESS VII**

"DISCOVER YOUR PASSIONATE PURPOSE TOGETHER"

The "Haircutter"	The Passionate Salon Professionals
36. "We are a bunch of individuals who go to work for ourselves. There is no team vision to unite us."	36. "We are one because we have one professional passionate vision."
37. "Basically we have to be on time for work. That's our biggest value, I guess."	37. "We are motivated by common values that we have taken the time to develop together. Our values unite our community to act in common ways."
38. Same as above	38. "Look at our salon flag that shows our visions and values that inspire us."
39. Same as above	39. "Do you want to hear our salon song that we sing for inspiration and motivation?

36

Create Your Salon's Passionate Purpose

"The only ones who reach their dreams are those who have them."

—Lew Losoncy

S tage Right Salon has taken the time to understand what it's passionate purpose is all about. "Service, service, service to people is what moves us," a proud stylist explained. "We are about people. When a customer needs a ride, we will pick you up. When a client is having difficulty losing weight we'll pull up some diets and encourage her to exercise. When someone talks about her great service she receives here, we invite her friend in to get to know every one of us. Our bulletin board has announcements of our customer's birthdays for the month. And, of course, proud achievements told to us or written up in the newspapers about our customers' families are always on the board. Service, service, service is our salon's passionate purpose."

NOTES

YOUR passionate purpose is your inspirational reason for being. Your passionate purpose goes deeper than your goals, although your goals, for example, your services and retail aims, are the result of fulfilling your passionate purpose. Your passionate purpose is deeper, because it ignites the fires, the reasons for being in your salon. Your passionate purpose is your shared dream. Consider some particularly inspirational passionate purposes:

"The United States is committed to placing a man on the moon and bringing him back safely by the end of the 1960's"

—President John F. Kennedy

"Our only reason to be here is to win the national championship."

—Notre Dame Football team, 1966

At your next staff meeting, take time to establish your passionate purpose together. Here is how to create your salon's passionate purpose.

"Today is a very, very important meeting. Today we will select one sentence that will describe what the passion is in the work we do within our salon community."

NOTES

Some questions to ask to stimulate thinking include:

1. Who are we?

2. What unique gifts do we have to offer (1) our customers, (2) our team, (3) our city?

3. What needs in the world can we meet?

4. What special knowledge and skills do we have?

5. How are we different?

6. What should we be grateful for?

7. What do we love doing?

8. What are we all about?

There are many, many passionate purposes. Some salons with whom we have worked to build their passionate purpose have incorporated (1) high energy, (2) great attitude, (3) service excellence, (4) fun, (5) high tech, and (6) teamwork into their passionate purpose.

Establish your passionate purpose and make sure that it is inspiring. Make copies for everyone and make a sign for your salon revealing to your customers what you are all about.

Our Salon's Passionate Purpose is

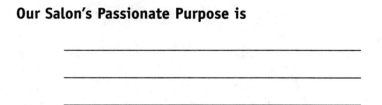

37

Understand The Passionate Values That Link Your Team

"When two people in a business always agree, one of them is unnecessary!"

—Joe Santy

Hi-Tek Salon in Bloomington, Indiana, the University City, does it as well as any salon community. Rebecca and her team love their profession and love developing their cultural values together. Hi-Tek has a customary ritual to celebrate the newest salon professionals' official arrival as part of the team. This moment has to be earned by a period of commitment to Hi-Tek's values. When the night arrives, the team heads off to TGI Fridays for dinner and the new team member's eyes are filled with hope, promise and pride. "I made it at Hi-Tek!" is a passionate, emotional expression of an experience that is not like just working anywhere. It's from the heart.

NOTES

YOU establish your passionate purpose together. Remember, the passionate purpose is a one sentence statement that inspires your team. Now you are ready to build your cultural values together. Our values are the ways we agree to act with each other here in our salon. Some salons that we have developed values with, have chosen values as varying as passion, respect, integrity, optimism, enthusiasm, teamwork, professionalism and encouragement.

Choose about 5 values and hold your staff meetings centering on a theme based on both passionate purpose and values.

Our Salon's Values are:

1. _____

2. _____

3. _____

4. _____

5. _____

Like Hi-Tek, put your values into action with rituals and fun. Make your passionate purpose and values important and meaningful.

* * * *

38

Have Fun Designing Your Flag That Shows Your Purpose And Values

"To love what you do, and feel that it matters. How could anything be more fun?"

—Kathryn Graham

The Great Hair Salon's passionate purpose was clear from the beginning of our teamwork program. "We are about one thing…high energy! We are upbeat, positive, and optimistic and every staff member knows this is a high-energy place. Our music is high energy, our people are high energy, and our clients are high energy when they leave. No one is sitting around here because everything is in motion, we are a model of change, growth and movement."

NOTES

Yes, it is obvious that Great Hair knows its shared passionate purpose and you can almost visualize the salon in your mind... and feel it in your heart. It was also interesting for every one at the teamwork program to see the flag that Great Hair would be presenting to the salons the next morning. Curiously, Great Hair's flag was the simplest one in the room. Only one symbol decorated the salon team's flag...a lightening bolt! " This is what we are about, high energy is as natural to us as lightening. We are going back to the salon after the teamwork program and design shirts with lightening bolts that will remind us constantly of our commitment to high energy!"

YOU have established your salon's passionate purposes and values. Now its time for you to bring those values into a visible form by developing your flag that represents your passionate purpose and values. Inspire your salon team to have fun developing the flag that will fly over your salon for years to come. And if you do like many salons do, you can incorporate it as part of your stationary and use it on tee shirts, coffee mugs or wherever your imagination takes you.

Start by taking your passionate purpose and values and ask if there are any symbols that can represent these ideas. Here are a few examples from salons previous teamwork programs.

Passionate Purpose or Values	Symbols
Teamwork	Hands Touching
Growing	Trees, Seeds
Overcoming Challenges	Salmon Swimming Upstream
Optimistic	The Sun
Vision	An Eye
Love	A Heart
Knowledge	A Book
Wisdom	An Owl
Openness, Diversity	Blending Colors
Customer Service	Hands Holding Hair Up
Determination	Ant Moving a Rubber Tree
Goal-Directed	A Finish Line
Retail Centered	A Retail Rack
Supportive	2 Hands High-Fiving

* * * *

39

Write Your Salon's Passionate Theme Song Together

"Coming together is a beginning, staying together is progress, and working together is success."

—Henry Ford

Remember TV's *The Addams Family* theme song? The family snapped its fingers to da da da da,...da da. Start snapping, like all of us did, for one's salon introducing the song the staff made up the night before.

Ready? "I'll bet you can guess... *da da*, We are the best... *da da*, When your hair is messed... *da da*, And feeling so stressed... *da da*."

Get the point? The song went on to include the salon's name. The song has been improved through the years but still continues to start off, and lighten up every staff meeting no matter how stressful the meeting may be.

NOTES

YOU are taking the time to build your culture together, something most small businesses never thought of doing. You have defined your collective passionate purpose that unites your team, and then you have identified five values that you agree to treasure and live by, you have created your own salon flag that reflects your purpose and values. There is one more important, and fun step involved in building your culture together. Writing your salon's theme song that reveals your purpose and values.

You can create your own music or melody, or, as most salons do, you may use an already existing melody, like *The Addams Family* song. I listened to salons play off such a wide variety of songs like, "We are family (using their salon's name)," to "(Salon's name) Rocky Mountain High," to "I want to hold your hand (do your hair), even to the tune of *Happy Birthday*, and *Bend Me, Shape Me*."

After selecting the music, go to your passionate purpose and see if it's possible to weave the theme in as the title or the overall climate of the song. Next work your five values into the song. Work on it until everyone is happy.

You are now ready. You are ONE, united by your salon's passionate purpose, common values, a flag that proudly waves over all of you, and your song. And when you go to recruit at the Beauty Schools, show the future cosmetologists how your salon is different. You know who your are. You are the passionate salon professionals!

* * * *

 PROCESS VIII

"VALUE YOUR COMMUNITY MORE THAN YOUR EGO"

The "Haircutter"	The Passionate Salon Professionals
40. "We have a prima donna in our salon who does what she wants to do. Yeah, morale is low."	40. "No salon professional is better than the whole team's vision and goals."
41. "When someone criticizes someone else in our salon, tension is felt everywhere."	41. "We value growing from each other's feedback, realizing that every tip you get can help make you a better person."
42. "Some stylists yell at others, sometimes even in front of clients."	42. "We have learned the skills to be assertive, rather than aggressive. Just by changing your approach when you are upset can make a big difference."
43. "Our salon is a bunch of isolated individuals who have to get their own clients."	43. "All of us together can do much more to fill up our salon's book."

40

Act Out of Your Salon Goals, Not Individual Egos

*"Big egos are big shields
for lots of empty space."*
—Diana Black

"A chain is only as strong as it's weakest link," is an old cliché but one that can be applied to ANY salon. Why? It's a fact; a salon is only as strong as it's weakest teammate. Believe it or not, sometimes that weakest link is one of the highest producers in the salon.

Consider Heads UP in Maine. Only six stations, employs twenty people, 12 stylists and 8 support staff, and grosses approximately two million a year.

Joan, their third top stylist has had a problematic attitude. For four years, she has been great with her own clients, but she has been progressively treating the rest of the staff and sometimes other team members condescendingly. She is not a team player, not a passionate salon professional.

NOTES

Joan abhors salon meetings because after all, she is now a top producer and doesn't need to follow salon guidelines. She rarely attends shows because her self-centered mind doesn't allow any new ideas in from any other source than herself. Lastly, when there is a negative incident concerning the salon, instead of neutralizing the damage being done, she perpetuates it. Joan doesn't realize the impact of her not standing behind the salon has (nor does she care).

Philip, the forward thinking salon owner, has watched as his marketing efforts won Joan new service income heights, while her attitude sunk to new lows. He had seen this situation before — especially since some stylists forget that their climb up the income ladder always involves others. The great support from the staff at Heads UP, along with a salon owner who partners with stylists to achieve their goals was the key to Joan's success.

Being compassionate, Philip decides to have one last talk with Joan, her dismissal on the horizon. He has been through the "negative weakest link" virus before. And he knows, if he lets it spread he could stand to lose a lot more than one stylist!

YOU have experienced the stylist who thought she was so much better than everyone. "Why should I have to go to staff meetings? Somebody like me who is booked up to five years doesn't need this stuff. Besides I'll just quit if you push me. Any salon in town would take me in a heartbeat."

One person on a big ego trip can hurt every other team member in the salon. Worse yet, the client senses the whole mood of resentment that exists in what should be the relaxing haven of the salon.

Its funny, but many well-intentioned salon owners and managers, in an attempt to encourage their staff, keep building the employee's confidence with constant praise. Soon the employee reaches a tipping point and believes she is better than anyone else forgetting that it was her salon team that gave her the confidence in the first place!

NOTES

PSP'ers don't bring their egos into the salon. They view their work as helping people to look great and to feel great, and to help their team be successful. That's how they get high. A satisfied client or a successful week with their team gives these passionate salon professionals joys way beyond themselves. They make team goals more important than their selfish ego's.

Here are a few ways that ego-thinkers differ from goal thinking passionate salon professionals:

EGO-THINKERS	GOAL-DIRECTED PSP'ers
Use my idea	Use the best idea
Credit taker	Credit giver
Blames	Corrects
Me	We
Talks about self	Talks about you
Competes	Cooperates
Brags	Applauds others

Let go of your ego. Find joy in your work, your clients and your team — not in a lofty view of yourself.

* * * *

41

Welcome Criticism As A Growth Seed

"What is important is not what happens to us, but how we respond to what happens to us."

—Jean Paul Sartre

"Cindy, my perm is way too tight, it's not what I asked for!"

"Dale, my family says this color makes me look like a clown, I know I told you I liked it when I left but I guess the lighting in the salon is different."

"Jeff, this cut is horrendous, it looked great when you did it, but now it looks like it was cut with a chain saw!"

We could fill a book with clients' comments like these for salons over the world. Anyone who tells you that they never get complaints lies about other things too! We all have a challenge even now and then.

NOTES

Let's take a look at how one of our friends, LeeAnne from Choices Salon and Spa handles criticism. Empowering a staff of thirty-five, the passionate salon professional still loves being behind the chair a few days a week. Lee Anne can be barraged at times with incidents or can have weeks of calm! You just never know. First LeeAnne's whole staff are trained and empowered to neutralize a criticism or complaint in whatever reasonable way they can. How do they do that? By asking the simple question, "What can we do to make you happy about this situation today?"

Should a situation appear to be irrational, LeeAnne or one of her salon coordinators steps in to assist. The goal is always to strive for client satisfaction and LeeAnne likes to be made aware of all client concerns. Whether it concerns the brand of coffee in the salon or the clients supposed fried head of hair – if the client thought it was important enough to verbalize it, LeeAnne wants to know about it and possibly address it!

The positives that materialize from a non-intimidating approach like this are crucial to the growth of the salon and its individuals.

YOU have seen the stylist who looses it when the manager makes a suggestion to help her, and she responds defensively or attacking back with, "Its not my fault! Its your fault the way you run this place." Or the stylist who flies off the handle when a client is

upset with a look and reacts with, "Your hair is impossible to work on."

Think of the last time you were criticized. Re-live it. Was your response ego-centered, or goal-centered? If it was ego-centered you had a vigorous emotional response, with feelings ranging from hurt and depression and a desire to retreat to anger and attack.

Now re-live that very same criticism out of being goal-centered. As you go over the experience again in your mind simply ask yourself, "How can I use these ideas to help me become a better person?" Take your time and assess what happens.

Our guess is that when you responded out of ego, you created painful emotions for yourself and really didn't get any information to help yourself. And when you responded out of being goal centered you avoided the pain and got right to the point of learning ideas to help you make yourself become an even better person.

Now for the hard part. Do you think that you could muster up enough goal-centered strength to thank the critic for taking her time, and taking a risk to help you?

Okay. We'll take a "maybe" now, but at least you did learn something from this criticism, as you can learn from every criticism.

NOTES

Here are 10 steps to practice now for the next time you experience criticism from someone.

1. Stay calm, breathe deeply.

2. Reassure yourself that everything is going to be okay.

3. Be aware of your whole body language, communicating that you are open and not defensive.

4. Smile, if possible telling yourself you are determined to learn something from the critic.

5. Don't miss the person's point just because the critic gets loud or doesn't have the skills in offering criticism.

6. Discipline yourself to listen to the whole story before responding.

7. Summarize what the critic is saying to yourself.

8. Tell the critic, "So what I am hearing is that you feel or you think that I...."

9. Use what you can use from the critic's suggestions.

10. Thank the critic.

* * * *

42

Resolve Problems By Being Assertive, Rather Than Aggressive

*"Anyone can hold the helm
when the sea is calm."*

—Publilus Syrus

Bridget left a ton of towels to be washed for Debbie's shift. It was not the first time, and Debbie was boiling inside! There were three assistants in this quaint, four station salon in New England. Debbie always thought she was being walked on by the other two assistants — Bridget being the worst offender!

Unfortunately, the salon owner is quite busy servicing her own clients, not noticing little problems unless they are pointed out. This out of balance situation, though it is a small dilemma in the overall scheme of things, is huge to Debbie. The red head Debbie is moving like a bull towards a meltdown with Bridget and the unsuspecting salon owner.

NOTES

The interaction and socialization with others that the salon has to offer is a great training ground for the passionate salon professional to hone their personal and people skills including assertiveness.

An assertive — as well as intelligent — person would have Debbie first have a one-to-one talk with Bridget. Approaching the topic by asking Bridget if there was something preventing her from being able to finish the work on her shift, as the excess towels were causing Debbie not to complete the work on her shift. If there was something preventing Bridget from completing her work, maybe the salon owner should be made aware of it to fairly remedy the situation.

Salons, no matter how small or how large need everyone to be assertive in a positive way — it's a given with each other, and the client is no exception! An assertive stylist might be asked to give a client a body perm on blue rods and agree. Later, if the client complained that it was "too tight," the stylist is left owning the problem. Think about it. An assertive stylist would have explained why the perm could not be done and would have avoided the problem all together.

Being assertive can eliminate the majority of stress in life and in the salon!!

YOU know that any time two people get together for extended periods of time, there will be conflicts. Even when they are in love and have selected each other!

The busy stressful salon is a natural source for conflicts to arise.

Conflicts need to be addressed or passive-aggressiveness will be a common response, one in which others just keep quiet and seethe or pout, get stubborn or procrastinate. Salons want to encourage responsible assertive behaviors where the problems are vented for the purpose of improving relationships, not for the purpose of venting their emotions or hurting someone else.

Think of the differences among timid, assertive and aggressive this way. When someone treads on your foot, you can continue to allow the person to dig in while you just get upset on the inside and smile on the outside (timid), or you can take the other person down (aggressive) or you can firmly look the other person in the eyes and say, "Get off my foot" (assertive). When we are being assertive, all we are demanding is our fair share, no more, no less.

Contrast the differences between being timid, assertive and aggressive (see table on the next page).

Remember, if you are having a problem with person A in the salon, avoid telling and getting persons B, C, D, etc. involved. Take responsibility to be assertive without needing other's support. And remember, as well, if you are upset with person A, and have not told person A directly, you cannot expect person A to know what the specific problem is.

TIMID	ASSERTIVE	AGGRESSIVE
"Die and let live"	"Live and let live"	"Live and let die"
Avoids expressing own needs	Expresses own needs and understands other's needs	Domineering, Only understands selfish needs
Willing to take less than a fair share	Wants what one deserves, no more, no less	Only concerned with self
Hurts self	No one is hurt	Hurts others
Avoidance, passive-aggressiveness, martyr	Active openness done in private setting to only the significant person	Sarcasm, public display and put down

Here are some practical approaches to the development of your assertiveness skills.

1. Start by pointing out something positive in the other person.

2. Address the most important point that you want to get across.

3. Discuss why the person's behavior presents a problem to you.

4. Avoid, "You should," but rather use, "I feel."

5. Sensitively listen to the other person's reaction.

6. Recommend a solution if possible.

7. Notice immediately any positive change.

8. Constantly remind yourself that the two reasons you are being assertive are (1) to get your fair share, no more, no less and (2) to improve your relationship.

* * * *

43

All Of You Together
Can Fill Up
Your Salon's Book

*"The people who get on in the world are the
people who get up and look for the
circumstances they want and, if they can't find
them, make them"*

—George Bernard Shaw

At Attitudes Hair Studio in Langhorne, Pennsylvania it is clear to every client that this is a salon that has a team-based culture. One of the first impressions a client receives is a sign that reads, "At Attitudes we work as a team. If you are having difficulties scheduling an appointment with your stylist or would like to try another team member's talents, please feel free to do so, as we encourage change and support each other."

Clients know that at Attitudes, each stylist is there for the salon, not just for themselves. And the salon

NOTES

climate at Attitudes is warm and welcoming for clients.

The secret to making this successful is that the stylists truly do help each other. For example, if a client of Joe's is in Roxanne's chair, he will spend a few moments explaining to Roxanne in front of the client what he has previously done. This puts the client at ease knowing that Joe is there and it easily weaves Roxanne's ideas in with his and the client's. It's a triple home run for everyone especially the salon!

YOU have a huge number of people that your salon team can creatively find ways to bring into your salon. Find a local telephone book and count the number of people on just one page. Multiply that number by the number of pages of listed names. Now double that number since each name represents, on the average, at least two people. These are your salon's potential clients if you work together.

We believe that it is important for each member of your salon team to think bigger than oneself and dream of ways to help the whole salon. All of you together can do much more than each of you can do alone. There are many benefits for a team to work together to help the total salon. For one, a team compliments each others' work helping each client to receive more than one positive comment about her new look. For another benefit to the team approach, it is clear from radio talk shows we do that many clients want to go to another stylist in the same salon, but don't want to hurt their current stylist's feelings. And, unfortunately for the salon, they go elsewhere. A team-based salon could have kept these clients. And a goal-centered, not an ego-centered stylist would be an encourager to her client to try another staff member.

Here are a few practical, every day ideas to help your team to fill up your salon's book.

1. Make a commitment to retain every client your salon currently serves.

The surest way of building your salon's clientele is to start by making a commitment to not lose any of your existing clients. After all, remember that you get so close to your clients that you physically touch them and you listen to their feelings and concerns about their hair, skin and nails. Using your encouragement skills can greatly increase the chances of retaining each client. And, when you feel that you are in a rut with a client, show what a big thinker you are and offer her the opportunity to try any of your salon's professional staff members. Keep that client coming to your salon!

2. Use your salon's current clients as referral sources for future clients.

One way of doubling your salon's clientele is to make a commitment to get one client from each current client coming into your salon. Word of mouth referrals are the most effective and it is easy to see why. It is probable that the clients currently coming to your salon are happy with your work and your personalities. After all,

NOTES

out of all of the salons in your phone book, they chose you! Their friends, relatives and coworkers trust them more than an ad in the newspaper. All you have to do is make it known to your satisfied client that you would be thrilled if she would consider having a friend come in for a free consultation. And listen closely as your client talks about a friend. Think to yourself, she is talking about someone who will soon be our client!

3. Share ideas together on how to build your clientele.

All of you together can do more than each of you can do alone. Have brainstorming sessions where each passionate salon professional brings one idea into the salon on how to increase clientele. Make sure that meeting has a mood of encouragement for every idea. When someone offers an idea, every person thinks of one way of building on it.

4. Expand your client appeal base by relating to a variety of age ranges and cultural backgrounds.

Its easy to relate to someone who is, "just like me." The passionate salon professional loves expanding her ability to relate to a more diverse clientele. One Melbourne, Florida stylist told us that she started to learn Spanish to be able to connect with an increasing number of Spanish speaking clients. Expand yourself as well by learning to understand the interests of both younger and older clients.

5. Associate and network with other professional, occupational and career groups.

The popularity of clubs such a Rotary, Kiwanis, Zonta and others is due not only to social and community fulfillment, but for business reasons as well. These clubs provide an opportunity for people to network with each other. While addressing a women's network group in Winnipeg, Manitoba, I (Dr. Lew) was struck with the enthusiasm they had for each other's businesses. There were hairstylists, real estate agents, teachers and many small business owners in the room. Each passed out their cards to other members and you could see the power of networking. Wherever you go and meet someone new from your city, see it as an opportunity in front of you. Passionate salon professionals meet a real estate agent and ask for the person's business card.

> "If I find that a client in my chair is moving and about to sell their house, I'll give them your card. And, by the way here's my card. If you sell a home to someone, I'd really appreciate it if you would give them my card."

6. Create opportunities to give your salon greater community exposure.

Today, more than ever, passionate salon professionals are becoming more active in their communities. It is quite common to see stylists on local or national TV, hear them on the radio or read about them in the newspaper. Ask the local school principals if you could talk to the students about the importance of grooming and

NOTES

NOTES

appearance. Make yourself available for local theater groups. Make styling presentations at your local clubs.

7. Compliment peoples' hair wherever you go. Show people you notice.

Wherever you go, especially at parties, compliment peoples' hair. And then add something like, "Have you ever tried wearing your hair this or that way?" giving them something to think about. Then subtly pass them your card.

8. Seek out and invite high-profile and respected members of your community into your salon.

You have a gold mine if you have a client who is very high profile coming to your salon. People like to go where the trend is, and you can create a trend. Consider doing the hair of the local cheerleaders or people who are frequently in front of crowds.

9. Advertise the 3 main benefits of coming to your salon.

Decide together what you consider to be the three main benefits to coming to your salon. Memorize these benefits and whenever the opportunity presents itself, you can passionately rattle off why your salon would be a great choice for clients.

"Haircutters" go to work to make money to pay bills. Passionate salon professionals have a plan to build their salon's future together.

* * * *

 # PROCESS IX

"PLAY WITH REALITY"

The "Haircutter"	The Passionate Salon Professionals
44. "We sit in the dispensary complaining about everything."	44. "The secret is to immediately accept anything you can't change."
45. "Some days everything seems to go wrong. You know how Murphy's law works."	45. "We have fun reminding ourselves that it is unlikely that bad weather, heavy traffic and late customers are not in a plot to get us."
46. "It was a catastrophe!"	46. "It was a minor inconvenience."

44

Quickly Accept That What Is, Is!

"Reality isn't what we think it should be or wish it to be or want it to be or what we think it must be or ought to be. Reality is much simpler than that. Reality just is!"

—Lew Losoncy

What Is Is!!! Isn't It! Janice loves to complain about her hair! She's been going to Brittany for twelve years (the operative words are twelve years). Brittany gets anxious every time she sees Janice's name in her book because of her complaining. Every four weeks Janice comes in for a color and cut, three times a year she gets a perm. On some occasions, she comes in for a blow dry. In other words, Janice is a BIG ACCOUNT for the salon and for Brittany!

The salon owner and various staff members have attempted to enlighten Brittany about the situation. They have all explained that if she's coming back for twelve years maybe, just maybe, she really is happy

NOTES

with her hair. The sad fact is some people just like to complain, (what is, is). Maybe they are missing a sympathetic ear in another corridor of their life!

The same holds true for the salon staff. All of us creative people have quirks — it's to what extent that makes some acceptable and other annoying. That also includes the physical aspects of the salon, we know a stylist that hated the mirrors and glass shelves (what is, is) in the salon, to the point of letting it eat away at her when she worked! Talk about wasted energy!!

The next time you're confronted with a situation, person, or thing that you know can't be changed, take a deep breath, exhale with a "what is, is" and keep your growth moving forward!

YOU have heard the most useless word in the English language. The word is, *should*. There are no *shoulds*, anywhere in the universe. *Shoulds* are grandiose statements by individuals demanding that the world be different than the way it in fact was. Listen to some of these absurd *should*, statements. And notice that every time we say the word *should*, we are getting ourselves upset, sometimes even producing frustration for ourselves.

"It *shouldn't* be this cold in June."

"I *shouldn't* get ten red lights in a row."

"My last client *should* have given me a bigger tip."

When you hear a *should* simply ask the other person what they think *should* be. For example if someone says, "I shouldn't get ten red lights in a row," ask him, "How many red lights *should* you get?"

REALITY IS NOT WHAT WE THINK IT SHOULD BE: REALITY IS WHAT IT IS!

Learn to remind yourself that, "What is, is! Let's practice.

You are in the salon on a busy Saturday during the holidays. Someone comes running into the salon to tell you that your car was just hit in its parking space. The driver hit and ran, leaving the car all banged up. You run out to your car and its barely drivable. Remember the three words you tell yourself. "What is, is!"

It's the hottest summer day in the salon you can remember and the air conditioning breaks down. And it was just repaired. You respond, "That shouldn't have broken down." And you remind yourself that, "Yes, that's exactly what should have happened. Why? Because it did! What is, is!"

Stress can be avoided by three simple words. What is, is! And remember, everything in a salon is the way it is — that is, until we change them. So instead of saying, "He, she or it should," save your frustration and simply ask yourself, "What's my plan!?"

* * * *

NOTES

45

The Universe Does Not Revolve Around Your Salon, Does It

"A hundred years from now it will not matter what my bank account was, the type of house I lived in, or the kind of car I drove, but the world may be different because I was important in the life of a child."

Jordan: *I'm running thirty minutes behind because Sheila was late.*

Jillian: *I understand, but Mrs. Sim wants you to see her hair before I shampoo her.*

Jordan: *I can't deal with all this. I'm not a machine.*

Jillian (Thinking): *Don't worry Jordan, keep acting this way in front of clients and when I have my chair, it's going to be extra easy for me to build my clientele from yours!*

NOTES

Two years later a lot of Jordan's clients had switched to Jillian. Jillian had a deep gratitude for anyone who sat in her chair and they knew it.

An interesting experience for you, the reader, might be to the pick up the dictionary and look up the word, "service." You'll notice that the extensive definition summarizes to be "helping and serving others."

When clients are late due to traffic, power outages due to storms interrupt salon activities, someone's child has a mishap right before their appointment, these are not conspiracies against you!

Things happen, the universe is fickle, the worst thing you can do is let it affect the treatment of those presently around you.

Give yourself a wake up call. Open the yellow pages under beauty in your area and see how many other salons your clients could have chosen — Jillian did!

YOU are beginning to get paranoid after you 9:00, 9:30 and 10:00 are no shows. You are already getting a little bit angry at your 10:30 who hasn't arrived yet. You are putting some pressure on her in your mind. "What is going on here?" you begin thinking. "Why is everyone late? Didn't they like the last look I gave them?" And then you realize something. It is unlikely that your clients — who — don't even know each other. They had a meeting this past weekend at where they decided to stop coming to you. Not likely. The universe doesn't revolve around you!

PSP'ers use humor to help them cultivate a healthy outlook. They realize that events in the universe are not arranged around them personally. Reality has more important things to do than gang up on you and your salon to cause you problems.

A humorous attitude helps you face inconvenient realities by assisiting you to humbly admit that events in the universe are not arranged around your salon personally. You can acquire that humorous attitude by giving yourself a reminder — by bringing a globe or map of the solar system into the salon. When things are getting frustrating, look at the globe and think about the six billion people living on the globe. Then observe the map and recall that light travels at 186,000 miles per second and there are still places that light hasn't gotten to yet. And then ask yourself the question, "Should we take these things that happened today in the salon personally?"

Remember the next time you're in a traffic jam, and cars aren't moving, just get out of your car, go up to the car in front of you, tap on the window, and ask the driver the question burning in your heart:

"Was this the only time you could have been out here? Why are you holding up someone important like me?"

Passionate salon professionals know that it's not all about them!

* * * *

46

"Re-Label" Tough Situations To Take The Sting Out Of Them

"All problems become similar if you don't dodge them, but confront them. Touch a thistle timidly, and it pricks you; grasp it boldly and its spine crumbles."

—William S. Halsey

Every mistake is a tough situation to the person who made it. To soften the feelings associated with it, look for ways to categorize it as a positive or make it smaller by using different self-talk.

Linda makes a mistake with a color and by the time the end of the day rolls around, you would think that she murdered someone. She beats herself and her talents into the ground. Tomorrow, she'll be correcting it but for now friends, family and small mammals better stay out of her way! Even once the color is corrected, the salon staff knows it will be another couple of days before her inner banshee subsides.

Diametrically opposite — and a situation that is truly serious (and not a mistake) is that of Arnie.

A visionary stylist for forty five years, Arnie who upon being diagnosed with a terminal illness immediately categorizes it as a "minor obstacle" on the road of life. He kept his upbeat attitude with this obstacle until the time of his death. To this day, his attitude still permeates the thoughts of his family and friends.

YOU have seen clients, and other stylists who could get themselves bent out of shape. As they talk, listen closely to the words they are choosing to use to get themselves riled up. "She makes me angry!" or I was devastated," or "That slayed me," are sure-fire indicators of a person's overreaction to situations. The very words are predicting that the individual is fueling up her engines to spin out of control. Re-labeling involves re-routing one's negative emotions by choosing to use different, less explosive words.

Words are biochemical triggers because the words we use stimulate our emotions. Words are one of our ways of telling others and ourselves how good or how bad a situation really is. Remember, a situation, or something that happens to us in life, is neither good nor bad, until we label it with words.

Have you ever noticed how some stylists, when upset, start flailing their arms, nearly exploding — especially when discussing one of their obnoxious clients?

Re-labeling is a self-empowerment strategy for a PSP and involves diminishing the power of a potentially frustrating or volatile situation by looking at the experience in a different way. You are re-labeling when you consciously select words that are less explosive, inflammatory and volcanic to describe your experience.

1. Recognize that events become for you whatever you label them.

2. Re-label setbacks as mere inconveniences.

3. Recognize that the most anything in life can be is an inconvenience, rather than a tragedy or a catastrophe.

4. If you fail at something instead of labeling the experience or yourself as failing or a failure, re-label the event as a learning experience. Simply ask yourself, "What did I learn?"

5. Practice using the following words frequently; inconvenience, nuisance and hindrance.

Practice re-labeling by finding less volatile and upsetting words.

• Instead of saying, "I failed," you might say, "_____ ."

• Instead of "I was rejected," you could say, "_____."

• Instead of "It was terrible, awful, horrible" you could say, "It was.........................."

• Instead of "We are done, finished, devastated," you might say, "We are lucky because now we can......................."

PSP
NOTES

Here are a few more examples that you as a PSP can employ to re-label and re-route pain.

ELIMINATE THESE WORDS	USE THESE WORDS
"I can't."	"I didn't in the past, but I will in the future."
"I'll try, but I know I'll never succeed."	"I am determined to."
"If only, then I could."	"It's up to me!"

Interestingly, you could re-label in positive ways as well. When someone asks you how your day is going, instead of saying, "OK, I guess," you could respond with animation, "It is going awesome!" You'll actually make yourself feel better because your positive emotions are triggered by your re-labeled words. You could experience it yourself today as, "never having been better!" And instead of being, "all right," the PSP may answer, "I'm turbo-charged!"

* * * *

 # PROCESS X

"FIND YOUR WAY TOGETHER"

The "Haircutter"	The Passionate Salon Professionals
47. "The stylists hate the manager."	47. "All of us try to understand the stresses that others have on the team."
48. "People in the salon are are good at spotting what's wrong with each other."	48. "We see what's right with each other."
49. "What are we going to do. We are helpless to sell retail or get more clients."	49. "Somewhere in our whole team's unlimited creative minds we can double our business in the next 5 years."
50. "You really can't change things here."	50. "We dream of what we can create out of our salon."

47

Respect Every Teammate's Roles And Responsibilities

"After all this is over, all that will really have mattered is how we treated each other."

The passionate salon professional has a respect and sensitivity to all the various roles a salon's staff compromises.

"Let's all try to understand and be a bit more sensitive to each other's pressures," the sympathetic salon owner Mrs. Brie suggests.

Martha, our cleansing tech has had only three days working in our salon and can sure use a little extra support. I loved the way Amber defended Martha with that client who was upset with her and challenged her competence at shampooing. "

NOTES

"And a few of our newest stylists are starting to develop their confidence at suggesting consultations and making professional recommendations. We might all think about that period of time it took us getting started and feeling comfortable with people."

"And Andrea our manager has the loneliest job of them all. While still styling she is responsible to make the bottom line, while still having time for customers, sales people and all of us. She gets less sleep than anyone. When you walk a mile in her shoes, its pretty tough."

"Wendy, what can I say? Wendy, as a receptionist you are the first lady of our salon. You are our traffic control artist and you hear complaints every day that you don't even bother us about. Let's all have a little more understanding of Wendy's huge responsibilities. OK guys?"

"Wait a second Mrs. Brie. Let's not forget about you," Amber chimes in. "You pay the bills, you gave us all jobs, you believed in us, you trained us, you encourage us to grow and get more education. And you are the only one here who put her money where her mouth is."

YOU are very well aware of the frustrations and stresses of your role on the salon team. You live these stressing experiences every day. And chances are outside of work you associate with people who do what you do. The secret that PSP'ers know is to take the time to understand the pressures, stresses and frustrations of others on the team. Take a few minutes and walk a mile in the shoes of every position in the salon to sensitize yourself to understand everyone's unique stresses, pressures and frustrations.

Write in at least three challenges each role faces.

NOTES

Receptionist _____

_____

_____

Cleansing Technician _____

_____

_____

Stylist _____

_____

_____

Specialist _____

_____

_____

Manager _____

_____

_____

Owner _____

_____

NOTES

At your next staff meeting share the ideas with each other discussing each role, one at a time. Ask each person in that role to summarize how well the rest of the salon team understands her pressures.

* * * *

48

Focus On Each Teammate's Strengths And Potential

*"You can't pick people up,
by putting them down"*

—Lew Losoncy

"Ganine never takes a foil," the pouting Virginia mumbled. "Ginny, did you ever see the beautiful precision cuts that Ganine does?" interjected an exuberant Casey. Casey continued in a sincere tone of voice, "Ganine has been styling hair longer than any of us, in her day frosting caps were the norm. Foiling was never her strength; she has admitted herself that her strength is in precision cutting and styling. The size of her book validates that, after all it takes six weeks to get an appointment with her."

A relentless Virginia, totally missing the point shoots back, "Well she should learn how to do them." Casey, attempting to enlighten her troubled teammate asks, "Did you ever consider how many foils Ganine has shared with the rest of the salon? I'd love a salon full of Ganines giving me foils all day long! You should know how it is Virginia, you hate to put hair up and usually book that with another one of us that loves it."

Virginia's slow smile suggests that she is reconsidering. "I guess you're right Casey; I wasn't seeing the whole picture. I guess I even profit from some of Ganine's clients. That's the beauty of our business, that by knowing our limitations and building on our strengths, we can make a great living!"

Casey and Virginia had hit the "aha" on the money! By understanding each others strength's and limitations, it allows a salon to function as a cohesive team. Any weaknesses in the salon's strengths would become invisible as passionate salon professionals would work synergistically picking up for stylists with a different skill set making sure every client's service was delivered seamlessly!

YOU have been on teams that were encouraging and others that were discouraging. What a huge difference. Discouraging teams dwell on shortcomings and mistakes, while PSP teams are energized as they center on each teammate's strengths, assets, potential, efforts, improvements and progress. PSP'ers are upbeat, spirited and, yes, passionate about each other's possibilities, and communicate by word and action that, "I believe in you, you can do it!"

Here are a few ways that discouraging teams differ from PSP teams:

DISCOURAGING TEAMS	TEAMS OF PSP
Centers on mistakes	Highlights positive actions
Quick to see what's wrong	Spotlights what's right
Destroys and pulls down	Constructs and builds up
Identifies liabilities	Identifies strengths
Finds why you can't	Discovers why you can
Thoughts limited to past experiences	Possibility thinker

Bring this PSP mood into your salon. Take some time to think about each of your teammates. Identify at least five strengths, assets, possibilities, talents, from people skills to attitude to technical skills. And then you will have an asset bombardment session with each other to bring out everyone's strengths and passion.

List each team member's name, include everyone.

1.

2.

PSP

NOTES

3.

4.

5.

6.

7.

8.

9.

10.

* * * *

49

Proceed As If Your Challanges Have Solutions

"The future is not a result of choices among alternative paths offered by the present, but a place that is created- created first in the mind and will, created next in activity. The future is not someplace we are going to, but one we are creating. The paths are not to be found, but made, and the activity of making them changes both the maker and the destination."

—John Schaar

"Sometimes our clients buy their retail styling products in the supermarket rather than in our salon," echoed the majority of the stylists at "Your Hair" salon. Their monthly meetings had turned into group blame sessions, focusing on why things couldn't be accomplished as opposed to using less energy finding how to turn a situation around.

Frank, owner of Your Hair decided it was time for a wake up call for all — including him! He is a self-improvement junkie, reading all kinds of books and attending seminars but he was lax in implementing what he learned from them. Today was his day to turn his knowledge into wisdom backed with action.

His training has taught him when faced with a challenge get to the root of the situation by asking targeted questions.

"What are your clients saying to you about seeing the products outside the salon?" Frank inquired. He went on, "What do you feel we should do about the situation?" "Is there anything we can do to put a positive spin on this?"

In this case, the main problem was the perception by the clients that buying the products outside the salon costs less than in the salon.

The staff agreed that they would rise above this challenge.

Gabs jumped up, "Let's go out and price those products at the drugstore and supermarket where our clients go. And we could post a cost comparison sign showing them that our product costs less."

Michele added, "And let's remind our clients, and we can even put it on our cost comparison sign that we guarantee our products here. The clerk at the supermarket doesn't know or care about their hair, does she?"

NOTES

Frank explains, "Great thinking guys, we're solving our challenge, rather than making ourselves miserable. Think about it, the product is diverted because it has value to our clients. If we can help them get this product they value at less, honor all competitors coupons and at the same time knowing their hair better than the clerk and caring for them, who wouldn't buy the professional product from their passionate salon professional?"

YOU give your salon a huge advantage just by acting as if every challenge has a solution. Think about it. Hasn't every achievement from the placing of the flag on the moon, to the curing of diseases, to the building of successful salons been accomplished by optimists, people who proceeded as if problems have solutions?

The same holds true for your salon. When facing any issue or challenge, instead of immediately getting frustrated, condition yourself to immediately think that somewhere in your collective minds and passionate hearts is not just one answer, but many answers to this challenge. You can trigger your optimistic feelings by looking up and shaking your determined head in a yes manner, rather than looking down and moving your head in a no way.

Consider the following challenge:

"Can we increase our color business by ten percent?"

Imagine how a "no" will work. A "no" gets us to use or mental resources in such a way as to guarantee no passion, or progress.

"No it won't work because people in our neighborhoods don't really want color. And if they wanted color, they would ask. And besides if we get pushy, they won't come back, ..."

Sense how just saying, "yes," up front, you bring out your passion and creative determination to find a way.

"Yes, we can increase our color business. We can start by putting up signs talking about color. We could color our own hair. We could think about each client at the beginning of the day and what an ideal color might be like for them and when they arrive discuss it with them. We could... ."

See the difference? Its starts right up front by putting yourself into a "yes, we can," mindset.

* * * *

50

Become "Could-Be-Ness Thinkers"

"What we will achieve inwardly, will change outer reality"

— Otto Rank

"Oh, its just soap in a bottle, what's the big deal," Darla whines.

"What? Darla honey, open your mind up to see all of the possibilities in that precious professional product now in your hands," her friend Belinda explains. "You see Darla, to most of your clients that bottle represents not only clean hair, but a cleaner feeling, and to some of your clients, the bottle gives them more confidence being dandruff free. To us stylists, it represents additional income and funding for our continued education and positions us as true professionals in recommending what is best for our clients. You see the words, 'professional product,' meaning you have earned the right to ethically recommend that bottle. The bottle makes you an expert. Shall I go on, Darla, because there is more."

"I just never thought about it that way, Lindy. I'm beginning to think that this professional product is under priced."

"Darla, would you like me to tell you about the power of our shears? They built my home for me!"

YOU can take any object in the salon, or in life, and add value to it just by looking at it, not just as it is, but as it could be. Take for example a pencil. If you read the dictionary definition of a pencil you'll see something like a rod shaped object filled with graphite or lead used for writing. If that's all you think a pencil is, that's all that it could be.

Take a few minutes a list everything that a pencil could be. Use your unlimited mind. No answer is wrong. Discover the could-be-ness in that pencil. For example, could be used to teach a child the color yellow, or could be used to scratch your back or protect yourself. Go!

1. _____

2. _____

3. _____

4. _____

5. _____

6. _____

7. _____

8. _____

9. _____

10. _____

Notice that while the pencil didn't change, the value of the pencil did. With each new idea as a could-be-ness thinker, you brought more value to that same old pencil.

Creating a "could-be-ness" mood amongst passionate salon professionals involves experiencing your salon, not as it is now, but as it could be. Let your unlimited creative minds flow with ideas. Accept every idea, no matter how crazy it might seem at first. Operate out of the mood that partial solutions are valued because they provide sparks for bigger solutions.

Add value to your professional services and retail. Add value to each other in your client's eyes. Add value to your salon. Think of five ways you could be a could-be-ness thinker and add value to some aspect of your salon.

1. _____

2. _____

3. _____

4. _____

5. _____

* * * *

NOTES

Congratulations!

You are connected to millions of other passionate salon professionals making the world a more beautiful place. You will always be:

1. Moving with a higher purpose,
2. Bringing your heart into the salon,
3. Building everything you touch,
4. Driven from within,
5. Available,
6. Taking each person one step at a time,
7. Finding your passionate purpose together,
8. Letting go of your ego,
9. Playing with reality and
10. Finding your way together.

And when some one asks you what you do for a living, look at them and simply describe that, "I cosmetically and psychologically transform self-images and destinies of fellow human beings. I'm a passionate salon professional."

Peace and Love,

Dr. Lew and Joe Santy

100 Thoughts to Bring Out Your Passion for Your Profession and Life

NOTES

20 PASSION-GENERATING REMINDERS TO MYSELF:

1. Ultimately what I do for a living is to help people feel good. I do that through my skills, my professional tools and products...and my attitude. When my clients look good, they feel great.

2. I don't just cut hair, but I give people courage and confidence and hope. Maybe the teenager in my chair today is thinking about asking someone out for a date. I help him develop his confidence. Perhaps I will have played a role in his beginning a new relationship.

3. Can any other profession claim that it gives gifts greater than courage, confidence and hope?

4. I touch people. Some of my clients may not be touched by anyone else in their lives. I cannot afford to be a cold person.

5. I can make a little child's day by telling her how pretty she looks after her style.

NOTES

6. Today I can bring a smile to an elderly woman's face by listening to the same story she tells every week — but I'll really hear it this time.

7. I can slow down the bulldozing client who comes in hostile at the world and tell her how nice of a smile she has.

8. I can design the young girl's hair today with the awareness that someday she might be asking me to do her hair for her wedding.

9. Hair that was genetically and environmentally determined by the history of a particular client, I can improve in an hour.

10. I can do a before and after of everyone I see today in my mind by observing how he or she looked when they came in and how he or she looked as they left. I was the difference!

11. I can suggest additional benefits to each one of my clients.

12. If I have free time, I can send out thank you cards to my clients. Imagine how they will feel as they think about our salon.

13. Only I can choose my attitude I take towards my clients.

14. I can look forward to an educational class coming up in the future and share what I will be learning with my clients to plant seeds in their minds about a new look.

NOTES

15. I am part of a network of passionate salon professionals who make the world a more beautiful place. With each new look, I add to our professional image in society.

16. I can feel proud.

17. This day I can learn ways to become a more passionate salon professional for the rest of my career.

18. I am creative.

19. I am able to see the results of my work as soon as its done, unlike most other professions.

20. I can change the world, client by client.

20 WAYS
OF BUILDING PASSION FOR OTHERS:

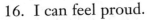

21. I will start every conversation with my clients by saying something positive about them. I'll be their salon stimulant.

22. I can forgive someone today and find a whole renewed life with them.

23. I can turn peoples' negative qualities into positive qualities. I can color drab hair or give bounce to flat hair.

24. With a client or another staff member, I can dream of even better ways of creating beautiful hairstyles.

25. I can say a long deserved, "Thank you," to someone who has taught me something, especially if I have taken him for granted.

NOTES

26. I can share my caring with someone in need.

27. Instead of talking I can choose to listen today.

28. I can trust again.

29. Today I will give credit to others, rather than take it.

30. I can help someone feel important.

31. I am determined to look beyond the tough person's surface and find a tender heart inside.

32. I can tell another stylist that I think she is really talented.

33. Rather than to compete, I can choose to cooperate.

34. I can turn a backbiting conversation into a positive one, thus gaining everyone's trust and respect.

35. I will sing.

36. I can write a poem to a co-worker.

37. I can understand the other side.

38. I can give the stylist next to me a big hug, for no reason at all.

39. I can smile enthusiastically and be the sunshine.

40. Today I will tell some one I love them.

20 IDEAS
TO STAY TURNED-ON EVEN WHEN
SOMEONE TRIES TO TURN ME OFF:

NOTES

41. No one chooses my attitude. I don't control what people say, but I do control my reaction to their words. I choose my attitude.

42. I can understand that people who say hurtful things are themselves hurting. I don't have to hurt myself by getting bogged down in the very game I find distasteful.

43. Instead of telling someone else to just be happy and starting a tug of war, I will go about in my own positive way and be an example.

44. Even if I don't like her mood, I can still enjoy the individual sitting in my chair.

45. I'll look at all of the positive aspects about myself when criticized.

46. Today I'll reflect on some of the proudest moments of my life.

47. I'll think about the three best things about myself.

48. I see why rejections are tough if I choose to believe that my value as a person is based upon the approval of others. However, I choose to believe that rejections can be helpful because they provide me with opportunities to sharpen my skills in dealing with others.

49. I can absolutely, totally, completely refuse to get down today, no matter what happens.

NOTES

50. When I get a break I can relax listening to some soft and upbeat music.

51. I can take a walk.

52. I can imagine where I will be in a few hours, not where I am now.

53. If the moment seems difficult, I will think of it as the low clouds on the horizon, beyond which lies the sunshine. I just have to look a little higher.

54. I can choose to compliment the person who just criticized me.

55. I will open up honest communication with others about areas where they are overstepping their boundaries with me.

56. I can ask another stylist for help with a hairstyle and help her feel more important.

57. I'll tell people what I like about them.

58. I can write someone a note at lunch time.

59. I will offer someone my help.

60. I will let people know that when I have a positive attitude, I feel better about my work.

20 THOUGHTS
TO TURN AROUND A TURN DOWN DAY:

NOTES

61. This is going to be my day, no matter what.

62. I AM ALIVE. This is my moment in the history of the universe. Let history record how I turned this day around.

63. Life will never give me more than I can handle. Apparently life really respects me some days.

64. The worst anything in life can be is a simple inconvenience.

65. I'm going to second gear myself out of this rut.

66. If we can put a man on the moon, I can overcome this setback.

67. I can actually laugh at this mess I'm in. I mean a real belly roll around on the ground laugh.

68. Things could be worse. I could be going through this experience and be thirty years older.

69. I have at least as much courage now as I did in the most courageous moments of my life.

70. What is, is!

71. In this situation, I'll accept the things I can't change and change the things I can.

72. I can take personal responsibility, rather than blame.

73. I'm making a plan to get on the outside of this negative geography.

NOTES

74. What about a nice warm bath?

75. How many free vacations can I take right here in my own home town? The park, the tennis court, the library, etc.

76. I will write my own positive horoscope for today, and then prove it right.

77. I can believe, rather than doubt.

78. With a lift of my chin, I will fire up my determination, feel a passionate surge in my heart and move forward.

79. I'll grin and bear it.

80. You know, there is almost nothing here in the salon I can't do. I can dream, choose, decide, create, invite because I AM ALIVE!

20 THOUGHTS TO STAY TURNED-ON AT HOME:

81. Each day I can look at the people around me in new and exciting ways.

82. I will thank people for the ordinary, everyday things they do for me.

83. Perhaps I can recall what attracted me to my friends in the first place and refresh my attitude towards them.

84. I can include others in my work.

85. I can leave notes at home so that when I'm away my family will still know I am thinking of them.

86. I will make some positive changes in my home environment to make me feel good.

87. I will read a positive book.

88. I can start jotting down positive quotes and post them throughout my home.

89. I will get some positive tapes to listen to at night.

90. I will watch less TV and listen more to soft music.

91. I'll stop reading the newspaper every day if it drags me down.

92. I am going to set new goals and dreams for myself.

93. I'll start an advertising campaign in my house to keep reminding me of my goals. For example, I'll put a sign on the refrigerator advertising the thinner me who will be appearing in a month.

94. I can consider all of the things I do have.

95. I can get enthusiastic about other peoples' lives.

96. I'll buy some roses and cook a special meal for someone acting as if I still have to really work to win someone over.

97. I can attempt to do something foolish to make another person laugh.

98. I'll clear my head.

99. I will live today as if it were my very first!

100. I am the major determiner of my life. And I determine it to be successful.

About the Authors

LEWIS LOSONCY

Dr. Lewis Losoncy is Matrix's motivational psychologist throughout most of the history of the company. He is the author of 19 books including *The New Psy-cosmetologists: Blending the Sciences of Cosmetology and Psychology* with Donald Scoleri, *The Motivating Team Leader*, *If It Weren't for You, We Could Get Along!*, and has developed the DVD *Passion for Beauty...Passion for Life!: Transforming Self-images and Destinies of People*, and the *Attitude Modification* DVD series.

"Dr. Lew" has spoken in all 50 US States, most of the Provinces of Canada and throughout Mexico, Australia, New Zealand, Thailand, as well as in England, France, Germany, Italy, Croatia and the Czech Republic. He has appeared on numerous TV programs including *CNN* and *CBS This Morning* and has been written about in print as varied as *The Wall Street Journal*, *Psychology Today* and *Prevention*.

He lives in Wyomissing, Pennsylvania with his wife Diane and daughter, Gabrielle.

* * * *

About the Authors

JOE SANTY

Joe Santy is an international guest artist for over thirty years, the majority being with Matrix Essentials. He has spoken in all 50 States, Canada, Mexico, Brazil, Grand Cayman, Germany, Egypt and Greece. Joe is the author of *Professional Permanent Waving— My Way* and co-author of *Perming Beyond Great Curl*. He is the co-inventer of the Cyberstyler Styling Brush and has been an on-air guest for QVC in the United States and Germany. He has appeared on New York One, CNN and CBS and his work has been featured in all of the US Beauty Trade magazines, as well as in consumer magazines. American Salon recently recognized Joe Santy as one of the beauty industry's legends.

Joe owns Atitudes Hair Studio in the historic borough of Langhorne, Pennsylania.

Joe lives in Yardley, Pennsylvania with his daughter Alexa and his dog Bella.

* * * *

References

Burns, David. *The Feeling Good Handbook*. New York, New York: William Morrow. 1990.

Csikszentmihalyi, Mihaly. *Flow: The Psychology of Optimal Experience*. New York: Harper & Row, 1990.

Losoncy, Lewis. *Attitude Modification*. DVD Series. Sanford, Florida. DC Press. 2004.

Losoncy, Lewis. *If It Weren't for You, We Could Get Along*! Sanford, Florida: DC Press, 2003.

Maltz, Maxwell. *Psycho-Cybernetics*. North Hollywood, California: Wilshire Books,1960.

Montagu, Ashley. *Touching. The Human Significance of Skin*. New York: Harper & Row, 1986.

Scoleri, Donald and Lewis Losoncy. *The New Psycosmetologists*. Reading, Pennsylvania, People Media, Inc. 1985.

How to Order
Books and DVD's

There are a couple of ways that you can obtain books and DVD's from DC Press.

- Call toll free 866-602-1476
  during business hours:
  (8:30 AM – 6 PM EST), M-F

- Visit our web site at:
  www.FocusOnEthics.com (24/7.)

- Fax any completed order forms to:
  407-688-1135 (24/7)

- Mail any completed order forms with
  appropriate credit card information or
  check to:

Order Department
DC Press
2445 River Tree Circle
Sanford, FL 32771